Maxim Hohmann

The impact of regulation on remuneration in banks

An analysis of EU, UK and German law

Anchor Academic
Publishing

Hohmann, Maxim: The impact of regulation on remuneration in banks. An analysis of
EU, UK and German law, Hamburg, Anchor Academic Publishing 2017

Buch-ISBN: 978-3-96067-075-9
PDF-eBook-ISBN: 978-3-96067-575-4
Druck/Herstellung: Anchor Academic Publishing, Hamburg, 2017
Covermotiv: © pixabay.de

Bibliografische Information der Deutschen Nationalbibliothek:
Die Deutsche Nationalbibliothek verzeichnet diese Publikation in der Deutschen
Nationalbibliografie; detaillierte bibliografische Daten sind im Internet über
http://dnb.d-nb.de abrufbar.

Bibliographical Information of the German National Library:
The German National Library lists this publication in the German National Bibliography.
Detailed bibliographic data can be found at: http://dnb.d-nb.de

All rights reserved. This publication may not be reproduced, stored in a retrieval system
or transmitted, in any form or by any means, electronic, mechanical, photocopying,
recording or otherwise, without the prior permission of the publishers.

Das Werk einschließlich aller seiner Teile ist urheberrechtlich geschützt. Jede Verwertung
außerhalb der Grenzen des Urheberrechtsgesetzes ist ohne Zustimmung des Verlages
unzulässig und strafbar. Dies gilt insbesondere für Vervielfältigungen, Übersetzungen,
Mikroverfilmungen und die Einspeicherung und Bearbeitung in elektronischen Systemen.

Die Wiedergabe von Gebrauchsnamen, Handelsnamen, Warenbezeichnungen usw. in
diesem Werk berechtigt auch ohne besondere Kennzeichnung nicht zu der Annahme,
dass solche Namen im Sinne der Warenzeichen- und Markenschutz-Gesetzgebung als frei
zu betrachten wären und daher von jedermann benutzt werden dürften.

Die Informationen in diesem Werk wurden mit Sorgfalt erarbeitet. Dennoch können
Fehler nicht vollständig ausgeschlossen werden und die Diplomica Verlag GmbH, die
Autoren oder Übersetzer übernehmen keine juristische Verantwortung oder irgendeine
Haftung für evtl. verbliebene fehlerhafte Angaben und deren Folgen.

Alle Rechte vorbehalten

© Anchor Academic Publishing, Imprint der Diplomica Verlag GmbH
Hermannstal 119k, 22119 Hamburg
http://www.diplomica-verlag.de, Hamburg 2017
Printed in Germany

Table of Contents

Abbreviations III

I. Introduction 1

II. Legislative Background 2

    1. Developments 2

    2. European Union Legislation 3

        2.1 Capital Requirements Directive 3

            2.1.1 Variable remuneration 4

            2.1.2 Termination payments 6

            2.1.3 Remuneration Committee 7

            2.1.4 Supervision 7

        2.2 Capital Requirements Regulation 8

    3. Legislation in the United Kingdom 9

        3.1 Limitation of remuneration 9

        3.2 Guaranteed variable remuneration 10

        3.3 Remuneration committee 11

    4. Legislation in Germany 12

        4.1 Limitation of remuneration 14

            4.1.1 Total remuneration limitation 14

            4.1.2 Sustainability in listed companies 15

        4.2 Report 16

    5. Future developments 16

III. Negative Impact of Regulation 19

    1. Costs 19

    2. Attractiveness of the market 19

    3. Common goods 20

IV. Necessity to regulate 22
    1. Risk exposure 22
        1.1 Remuneration 23
            1.1.1 Variable remuneration 23
            1.1.2 Allowances 25
        1.2 Supervision 27
            1.2.1 Credit Rating 28
            1.2.2 Internal supervision 29
            1.2.3 High earners 30
    2. Stability of the Financial System 31
    3. Protecting the public 34
V. Alternative regulatory proposal 35
VI. Conclusion 37
Bibliography V
    Articles V
    Books IX
    Statutory Provisions XII
    Others XIV

Abbreviations

Abs	Absatz (German for paragraph)
AG	Die Aktiengesellschaft*
AktG	Aktiengesetz
AuR	Arbeit und Recht*
BGBl	Bundesgesetzblatt (German HMSO)
BT-Drs	Bundestagsdrucksache
CFO	Chief Financial Officer
ch	chapter
CRD	Capital Requirements Directive
CRR	Capital Requirements Regulation
DB	Der Betrieb*
DrittelbG	Drittelbeteiligungsgesetz (German law on co-determination for medium sized companies)
DStR	Deutsches Steuerrecht*
DVBl	Deutsches Verwaltungsblatt*
EBA	European Banking Authority
edn	edition
ESMA	European Security and Markets Authority
EU	European Union
EUR	Euro
FCA	Financial Conduct Authority
FSB	Financial Stability Board
GG	Grundgesetz (German Constitution)
HMSO	Her Majesty's Stationery Office
IRZ	Zeitschrift für Internationale Rechnugnslegung*
JZ	Juristen Zeitung*
KSzW	Kölner Stift zum Wirtschaftsrecht*
KWG	Kreditwesengesetz (German Banking Act)
MitbestG	Mitbestimmungsgesetz (German law on co-determination for large companies)
no	number

NZG	Neue Zeitschrift für Gesellschaftsrecht*
para	paragraph
Plc	Public limited liability company
PRA	Prudential Regulation Authority
S	Seite (German for page)
S&P	Standard & Poor's
SYSC	Senior management arrangements, Systems and Controls
vol	volume
WiVerw	Wirtschaft und Verwaltung*
ZBB	Zeitschrift für Bankenrecht und Bankwirtschaft*
ZfU	Zeitschrift für Umweltpolitik & Umweltrecht*
ZHR	Zeitschrift für das gesamte Handels- und Wirtschaftsrecht*
ZIP	Zeitschrift für Wirtschaftsrecht*
ZRP	Zeitschrift für Rechtspolitik*

*German law journal

I. Introduction

'Excessive risk-taking (...) in banks (...) contributed to the failure of financial undertakings and to systemic problems in the Member States and globally'.[1] Both issues spread to other parts of the economy, causing tremendous costs for the public. Inappropriately designed remuneration systems in financial institutions are reported to induce such risk-taking.[2]

The EU regulators intervened to control risks through legislative measures.[3] Those measures have been differently implemented by Member States, making some European markets more attractive for bankers than others. Furthermore, the EU legislation is restricting banks' freedom of business, with possible negative effects of competition among global financial markets. Even though this book will show both supporting and objecting arguments towards bankers' remuneration, it will eventually refute the thematic statement, and argue that the regulation of bankers' remuneration is (mainly) necessary and justified to protect common goods of a sound functioning financial market. Nevertheless, some legislative provisions' effectiveness will be challenged.

This book will critically analyse the legislation of bankers' remuneration and detail relevant differences. Firstly, after a brief summary of past developments, EU legislative measures will be discussed. Then the part will be followed by an analysis of implementation methods of these measures in the UK and Germany. Furthermore, it is proved that the consequential negative impacts of such regulations are outweighed by overall positive effects. Accordingly, future development in regulating banker's remuneration is presented in short. Finally, an alternative regulatory proposal with a different approach to the existing law is considered.

---

[1] Commission Recommendation (2009/384/EC) of 30 April 2009 on remuneration policies in the financial services sector [2009] L 120/22 preamble recital (1).
[2] CRD IV preamble recital (62); Commission (n 1) recital (2).
[3] Brad Rice and Lorraine Johnston, 'Bankers' Bonuses Back in the Spotlight' [2014] 38 CSR 1, 1.

II. Legislative Background

1. Developments

The financial crisis, between 2007 and 2009,[4] occurred partly due to inappropriate remuneration policies in banks.[5] Banks or credit institutions are financial intermediaries in the payment system which collect money '(...) from the public and (...) grant credits for their own account'.[6] The European Commission published recommendations with regards to directors' remuneration,[7] addressing the issue of inappropriately designed management remuneration,[8] '(...) since the potential for abuse and conflicts of interests is essentially located there',[9] long before the crisis had occurred. Only a minority of Member States had implemented at least half of the recommendations.[10] Unregulated remunerations in the financial sector exposed serious weaknesses, such as short-term thinking among bankers to raise own compensation, without deliberating the corresponding risks.[11] To control such risks and to prevent a future financial crisis, legislative measures regarding banker's

---

[4] Larisa Dragomir, *European Prudential Banking Regulation and Supervision: The legal dimension* (Routledge 2012) 41; Rosa M Lastra and Geoffrey Wood, 'The Crisis of 2007-09: Nature, Causes and Reactions' [2010] J Int Economic Law 13 (3), 531.

[5] EBA, 'EBA Report on the application of Directive 2013/36/EU (Capital Requirements Directive) regarding the principles on remuneration policies of credit institutions and investment firms and the use of allowances' [2014] EBA Report from 15 October 2014 <https://www.eba.europa.eu/documents/10180/534414/EBA+Report+on+the+principles+on+rem uneration+policies+and+the+use+of+allowances.pdf> accessed 11 May 2016, ch I, para 3; CRD IV preamble para (51); Norbert Röttgen and Hans-Georg Kluge, 'Nachhaltigkeit bei Vorstandsvergütungen' [2013] NJW 900; Dragomir (n 4) 19; Barbara Deilmann and Sabine Otte, 'Auswirkungen des VostAG auf die Struktur der Vorstandsvergütung' [2009] GWR 261.

[6] Article 4 (1)(1) CRR; Article 3 (1)(1) CRD IV, Mathias Dewatripont and Jean Tirole, *The Prudential Regulation of Banks* (The MIT Press 1994) 13.

[7] Commission Recommendation (2004/913/EC) of 14 December 2004 fostering an appropriate regime for the remuneration of directors of listed companies [2004] OJ L385/55 and Commission Recommendation (2005/162/EC) of 15 February 2005 on the role of non-executive or supervisory directors of listed companies and on the committee of the (supervisory) board [2005] OJ L52/51.

[8] Preamble recital (1) Commission Recommendation (2004/913/EC) of 14 December 2004 fostering an appropriate regime for the remuneration of directors of listed companies [2004] OJ L385/55.

[9] Commission Recommendation of 30 April 2009 complementing Recommendations 2004/913/EC and 2005/162/EC as regards the regime for the remuneration of directors of listed companies OJ L 120/28 preamble recital (2); Preamble recital (13) Commission Recommendation (2005/162/EC) of 15 February 2005 on the role of non-executive or supervisory directors of listed companies and on the committee of the (supervisory) board [2005] OJ L52/51.

[10] Commission Report (COM (2010) 285 final) of 2 Mai 2010 on the application by Member States of the EU of the Commission 2009/385/EC Recommendation (2009 Recommendation of directors' remuneration) complementing Recommendations 2004/913/EC and 2005/162/EC as regards the regime for the remuneration of directors of listed companies 3.

[11] CRD IV preamble recital (62); Lucian A Bebchuk and Jesse M Fried, 'How to tie equity compensation to long-term results' [2010] Journal of Applied Corporate Finance Vol 22 No 1, 99; Lastra and Wood (n 4) 541.

remuneration have been introduced.[12] Following the Capital Requirements Directive (CRD) III,[13] which first dealt with issues of pay, its successor – the CRD IV[14] is currently in effect, regulating managers' remuneration.[15] The following part will explain relevant European provisions. The relevant UK and German rules will be cited as well, to avoid repetition in succeeding chapters.

2. European Union Legislation

2.1 Capital Requirements Directive

The CRD IV aims to regulate remuneration policies and practices on a consistent basis with an effective risk management.[16] Banks shall take '(…) into account national criteria on wage setting (…) [and make] a clear distinction between'[17] fixed remuneration, which is based on staffs expertise,[18] and 'variable remuneration which should reflect a sustainable and risk-adjusted performance (…)'.[19] A remuneration policy is appropriate when it ensures the long-term sustainability of a company based on pay for achievement.[20]

---

[12] CRD IV preamble recital (62); Avinash D Persaud, 'A ticking time bomb: TLAC and other attempts to privatise bank bail-outs' [2016] 3 JIBFL 160; Markus Weber, '§ 87' in Wolfgang Hölters (ed) *Aktiengesetz: AktG Kommentar* (2nd ed, C H Beck Verlag 2014) § 87 para 30; Hans-Christoph Ihrig and Carsten Schäfer, *Rechte und Pflichten des Vorstands* (Dr. Otto Schmidt Verlag 2014) 92; Rice and Johnston (n 2) 1; Bradley Rice, 'Allowances: Fixed or Variable Pay?' [2014] 38 CSR 17, 136; Hans-Ulrich Wilsing and Carsten A Paul, 'Reaktionen der Praxis auf das Nachhaltigkeitsgebot des § 87 Abs. 1 Satz 2 AktG – Eine erste Zwischenbilanz' [2010] GWR 363; Commission Recommendation of 30 April 2009 complementing Recommendations 2004/913/EC and 2005/162/EC as regards the regime for the remuneration of directors of listed companies OJ L 120/28; Barbara Dauner-Lieb, 'Die Verrechtlichung der Vorstandsvergütung durch das VostAG als Herausforderung für den Aufsichtsrat – Methodische Probleme im Umgang mit Rechtsunsicherheit' [2009] Der Konzern 583, 586; Holger Fleischer, 'Das Gesetz zur Angemessenheit der Vorstandsvergütung (VostAG)' [2009] NZG 801, 802; Gregor Thüsing, 'Das Gesetz zur Angemessenheit der Vorstandsvergütung' [2009] AG 517, 520; The Guardian, 'G20 leaders map out new economic order at Pittsburg summit' (The Guardian, 26 September 2009) <www.theguardian.com/world/2009/sep/25/g20-summit-economy-bonuses-deficits> accessed 11 May 2016; Council of the European Union for Economic and Financial Affairs press release of the 2911th Council meeting on 2 December 2008, 2.
[13] Directive 2010/76/EU of 24 November 2010 amending Directives 2006/48/EC and 2006/49/EC as regards capital requirements for the trading book and for re-securitisations, and the supervisory review of remuneration policies OJ L329/3.
[14] Directive 2013/36/EU of 26 June 2013 on access to the activity of credit institutions and the prudential supervision of credit institutions and investment firms, amending Directive 2002/87/EC and repealing Directives 2006/48/EC and 2006/49/EC OJ L176/338.
[15] EBA (n 5) ch I, para 1.
[16] CRD IV preamble recital (62); in Germany: para 4.2.3 second paragraph DCGK.
[17] CRD IV Article 92 (2)(g).
[18] CRD IV Article 92 (2)(g)(i); EBA (n 5) ch I, para 24 and 27.
[19] CRD IV Article 92 (2)(g)(ii) and preamble recital (64); para 4.2.3 second paragraph DCGK.
[20] Commission Report (n 10) 2; in the UK: SYSC 19D.3.8 R; in Germany: § 87 Abs 1 S 1 AktG; para 4.2.3 second paragraph DCGK.

2.1.1 Variable remuneration

The variable component of remuneration is linked to the employees and banks performance,[21] and take '(...) financial and non-financial criteria into account',[22] for a timeframe over several years.[23] Guaranteed variable remuneration is not permitted under the principle of pay-for-performance,[24] and shall only be given in exceptional circumstances, e.g. hiring new staff.[25]

The total amount of fixed and variable remuneration payable to a banker shall be appropriately balanced,[26] based on a ratio set by the bank.[27] However, that ratio limits the variable component to 100 per cent of the fixed remuneration.[28] Member States shall have the capability to set a lower maximum percentage,[29] but may also allow shareholders of the bank to approve a variable remuneration between 100 and 200 per cent of the fixed remuneration.[30] Moreover, Member States may have the power to set stricter requirements.[31] In the process of approving a higher ratio, the bank shall provide a detailed recommendation to its shareholders,[32] who vote by a majority of at least two-third, provided that 50 per cent of share-capital is present.[33] If less capital is present an extraordinary resolution is required.[34] Employees, who are directly concerned by the vote, shall have no voting rights if they hold shares in the bank of their employment.[35]

---

[21] Commission (n 9) preamble recital (2)
[22] CRD IV Article 94 (1)(a); Commission (n 9) preamble recital (6); in the UK SYSC 19D.3.39.
[23] CRD IV Article 94 (1)(b); in the UK: SYSC 19D.3.8 R, 19D.3.30 G (1) and (2) and 19D.3.43 R; in Germany: para 4.2.3 second paragraph DCGK; CRD IV Article 94 (1)(b) and preamble recital (63); Commission (n 9) preamble recital (6); Commission Report (n 10) 3.
[24] CRD IV Article 94 (1)(d), in the UK: SYSC 19D.3.44 R.
[25] CRD IV Article 94 (1)(e).
[26] CRD IV Article 94 (1)(f), in the UK: SYSC 19D.3.48 R (1).
[27] CRD IV Article 94 (1)(g); para 4.2.3 second paragraph DCGK.
[28] CRD IV Article 94 (1)(g)(i); Rice (n 12) 136; EBA (n 5) ch I, para 1; in the UK: SYSC 19D.1.3 R (2) and 19D.3.48 R (3); in Germany § 25 a Abs 5 S 2 ff KWG.
[29] CRD IV Article 94 (1)(g)(i).
[30] CRD IV Article 94 (1)(g)(ii); Rice (n 12) 136; EBA (n 5) ch I, para 1 and 7; in the UK: SYSC 19D.1.3 R (2) and 19D.3.49 R (1) and (2); Commission (n 9) preamble recital (10).
[31] CRD IV preamble recital (65).
[32] CRD IV Article 94 (1)(g)(ii) second paragraph, first point, in the UK: SYSC 19D.3.50 R (2).
[33] CRD IV Article 94 (1)(g)(ii) second paragraph, second point, in the UK: SYSC 19D.3.50 R (5) (a) and (b).
[34] CRD IV Article 94 (1)(g)(ii) second paragraph, second point, in the UK: SYSC 19D.3.50 R (5) (a) and (b).
[35] CRD IV Article 94 (1)(g)(ii) second paragraph, sixth point in the UK: SYSC 19D.3.50 R (4).

Member States may allow banks in their own national law to offer a discount rate of up to maximal 25 per cent of the total variable remuneration if the latter is deferred for at least five years.[36] The limitation of the total variable remuneration and the involvement of shareholders shall ensure that there is no incentive for excessive risk-taking and allow banks to design remuneration in accordance with its own needs,[37] but ensure that risks for the public are foreseeable and under control.[38]

The variable remuneration shall be paid based on the employee's performance.[39] To measure such performance future achievement and current risks as well as costs of capital and the liquidity have to be taken into consideration.[40] The component of variable remuneration shall be structured in a way that at least 50 per cent contain of shares or share-linked instruments,[41] or additional "tier 1 or 2 capital"[42] instruments, deferred for at least three to five years.[43] However, the variable remuneration, including the deferred part, shall only be paid if the bank has a sustainable financial situation and if the remuneration is justified based also on the bank's performance.[44]

The variable remuneration is not justified if the employee's actions led to a serious loss for the bank,[45] or it fails to comply with "standards of fitness and propriety".[46] In those cases, the whole '(...) variable remuneration shall be subject to malus or

---

[36] CRD IV Article 94 (1)(g)(iii) and recital (65); in the UK: ,SYSC 19D.3.52 R.
[37] CRD IV Article 92 (2) and preamble recital (66); SYSC 19D.2.2 G (2); Commission (n 9) preamble recital (3).
[38] CRD IV preamble recital (65).
[39] CRD IV Article 92 (2)(g)(ii) and Article 94 (1)(a) and (b); CRD IV preamble recital (63) and (64); Commission Report (n 10) 3; Commission (n 9) preamble recital (6).
[40] CRD IV Article 94 (1)(j) and (k); in the UK: SYSC 19D.3.23 R.
[41] CRD IV Article 94 (1)(l)(i) and (2); , in the UK: SYSC 19D.3.56 R.
[42] Tier 1 capital is the bank's core capital and Tier 2 capital is one part of supplementary capital (shared with Tier 3), all used to determine whether or not a bank has "sufficient eligible capital", taking into account the overall credit risk Frans De Weert, *Bank and Insurance Capital Management* (John Wiley and Sons Ltd 2011) 55; Francesco Saita, *Value at Risk and Bank Capital Management: Risk Adjusted Performances, Capital Management and Capital Allocation Decision Making* (Academic Press 2010) 9-10 (with a good explanation what is included in different capital types); Hennie van Greuning and Sonja Brajovic-Bratanovic, *Analyzing Banking Risk: A Framework for Assessing Corporate Governance and Risk Management* (3rd edn, World Bank Group Publications 2009) 157; D R Carmichael and others, *Accountants' Handbook: 2 Volume Set/Special Industries and Special Topics* (10th edn, John Wiley & Sons 2003) chapter 31, 12.
[43] CRR Article 52 (1) and 63; CRD IV Article 94 (1)(l)(ii) and Article 94 (1)(m).
[44] CRD IV Article 94 (1)(n); in the UK: SYSC 19D.3.27 R and 19D.3.61 R (1).
[45] CRD IV Article 94 (1)(n) paragraph 3 (i), in the UK: SYSC 19D.3.29 R (1).
[46] CRD IV Article 94 (1)(n) paragraph 3 (ii).

clawback arrangements'.[47] Bankers shall not circumvent the regulation for variable remuneration by taking other measures to "undermine the risk alignment effects"[48] or use vehicles that are not regulated in the CRD IV or CRR.[49] The CRD IV limits the variable remuneration of staff with a considerable impact on the risk profile to make financial institutions risk resistant.[50] The remuneration policy should, therefore, reflect "sound and effective risk management",[51] taking into account the banks "long-term interests".[52]

2.1.2 Termination payments

Termination payments, also called "golden parachutes", should be only a safety net if the contract of a director is canceled early, but not a reward for failure or misconduct.[53] Therefore, termination payments shall have a cap on the amount of two years' annual remuneration paid beforehand and should not be paid if a director leaves because of insufficient performance or for his own account.[54] Precluded are termination payments based on a change in the strategy of the company or in a merger and/or takeover situation, which led to the cancellation of the directors' contract.[55]

---

[47] CRD IV Article 94 (1)(n) paragraph 3, in the UK: SYSC 19D.3.29 R (2).
[48] CRD IV Article 94 (1)(p); in the UK: SYSC 19D.3.32 R; in Germany para 4.3.2 DCGK; Standard 14 of FSB Principles for Sound Compensation Practices (Implementation Standards) of 23 September 2009 <http://www.fsb.org/wp-content/uploads/r_090925c.pdf?page_moved=1> accessed 11 May 2016.
[49] CRD IV Article 94 (1)(q); in the UK: SYSC 19D.3.34 R.
[50] Rice (n 12) 136.
[51] CRD IV Article 74 (1), 92 (2)(a) and 94 (1)(d); EBA (n 5) ch I, para 38 and 39; Rice (n 12) 136; SYSC 19D.1.6 G (1), 19D.2.1 R and 19D3.7 R.
[52] CRD IV Article 92 (2)(b); in the UK: SYSC 19D.3.8 R.
[53] CRD IV Article 94 (1)(h); Commission (n 1) recital (16); Commission (n 9) preamble recital (7); SYSC 19D.3.54 R.
[54] para 4.2.3 fourth paragraph DCGK; Commission (n 9) preamble recital (7).
[55] Commission (n 9) preamble recital (7).

2.1.3 Remuneration Committee

The bank shall set up a remuneration committee.[56] Members of the committee shall not be influenced in their work by an inappropriate remuneration policy.[57] The committee shall have a chair and members, who are all members of the management body[58] without executive functions,[59] and are independent as well as adequately trained, to avoid insufficient incentives for risk in the bank's risk, capital or liquidity.[60] The committee shall ensure that the '(…) long-term interests of shareholders, investors and other stakeholders', as well as the public interest, are secured.[61]

2.1.4 Supervision

Competent authorities must ensure that '(…) institutions at group, parent company and subsidiary levels, including those established in offshore financial centers', comply with the rules of CRD IV regarding remuneration practices,[62] in order to '(…) secure and foster financial stability within the European Union'.[63] The evasion of the directives' provisions shall be prevented. Therefore, "risk of excessive leverage"[64] must be supervised. Information of bankers being remunerated EUR one million or more per financial year must be collected,[65] divided in business area and risk profile of the staff.[66]

Adequate remuneration policies are crucial to set the right incentives for banks' risk profile.[67] Information on natural person that are remunerated more than EUR one

---

[56] CRD IV Article 92 (2)(f) and Article 95; in Germany: para 5.3.2 DCGK; Commission (n 9) preamble recital (2); Commission Recommendation (2005/162/EC) of 15 February 2005 on the role of non-executive or supervisory directors of listed companies and on the committee of the (supervisory) board [2005] OJ L52/51, preamble recital (9).
[57] CRD IV Article 92 (2)(e); in the UK: SYSC 19D.3.15 R (3)(a) and (b), SYSC 19D.3.9 R; in Germany: para 4.3.3 and 5.4.1 DCGK; Commission (n 9) preamble recital (11).
[58] Article 3 (1)(7) CRD IV; Article 4 (1)(9) CRR.
[59] CRD IV Article 95 (2).
[60] CRD IV Article 95 (1); in Germany: para 5.4.5 second paragraph DCGK; Röttgen and Kluge (n 5) 900.
[61] CRD IV Article 95 (2); in Germany: para 5.5 DCGK.
[62] CRD IV Article 92(1); CRD IV preamble recital (67); Commission (n 9), preamble recital (2).
[63] CRD IV preamble recital (67); EBA (n 5) ch I, para 7.
[64] CRD IV Article 87(1).
[65] CRR Article 450 (1) (g), (h) and (i); CRD Article 75 (3); Regulation of 4 March 2014 supplementing Directive 2013/36/EU of the European Parliament and of the Council with regard to regulatory technical standards with respect to qualitative and appropriate quantitative criteria to identify categories of staff whose professional activities have a material impact on an institution's risk profile [2014] OJ L 167/30, preamble recital (12); in Germany § 24 Abs 1a Nr 8 KWG.
[66] CRD IV Article 75 (1) and (3).
[67] EBA (n 5) ch I, para 3; Röttgen and Kluge (n 5) 900.

million per financial year shall be forwarded to EBA and published.[68] Member States shall nominate a competent authority within their territory,[69] which has '(...) expertise, resources, operational capacity, power and independence necessary to carry out the functions relating to prudential supervision (...)'.[70] Competent authorities must ensure that bankers with a high-risk hazard comply with the rules regarding remuneration, in a manner which is not burdensome for the institution.[71] The management body in its supervisory function shall adopt independent internal reviews at least annually.[72] Such external monitoring will be necessary as the management cannot always control itself, due to conflicts of interests.

2.2 Capital Requirements Regulation

Banks shall under the Capital Requirements Regulation (CRR)[73] disclose information regarding remuneration practices and policy for employees which have an important impact on the banks' risk profile.[74] Transparency and disclosure are important to ensure good remuneration practice.[75] Such information includes details about the determination of remuneration,[76] performance criteria,[77] design of the remuneration system and how it measures '(...) risk adjustment, deferral policy and vesting criteria',[78] ratio between variable and fixed remuneration,[79] how the performance is linked to share or other options,[80] and how the scheme for variable components of remuneration is structured.[81] The number of individuals earning more than EUR one million per financial year also has to be disclosed.[82] However, Member States or their competent authorities can request information of the total remuneration for a member

---

[68] CRD Article 73 (3).
[69] CRD IV Article 4 (1).
[70] CRD IV Article 4 (2).
[71] CRD IV Article 92 (2); in the UK: SYSC 19D.3.4 R (1)(a).
[72] CRD IV Article 92 (2)(c) and (d); in the UK: SYSC 19D.3.10 R.
[73] Regulation (EU) No 575/2013 of 26 June 2013 on prudential requirements for credit institutions and investment firms and amending Regulation (EU) No 648/2012 OJ L176/1.
[74] CRR Article 450 (1) and CRR preamble (97).
[75] CRR preamble recital (97); Commission Report (COM (2009) 114 final) of 3 March 2009 Communication for the spring European Council – Driving European Recovery Volume 1, 4.
[76] CRR Article 450 (1)(a).
[77] CRR Article 450 (1)(b).
[78] CRR Article 450 (1)(c).
[79] CRD IV Article 94 (1)(g), CRR Article 450 (1)(d).
[80] CRR Article 450 (1)(e).
[81] CRR Article 450 (1)(f).
[82] CRR Article 450 (1)(i).

of a bank's management.[83] If the bank is significant in size and complexity, unspecified information about the total remuneration of the management body shall be made public.[84] By disclosing such information to all relevant stakeholders, the bank's risk associated with remuneration is ensured to be under control and transparent to the market.[85] Disclosure furthermore enhances compliance with the regulations of remuneration.

3. Legislation in the United Kingdom

In the United Kingdom, the FCA introduced the Remuneration Code ("the code"),[86] regulating 26 largest banks.[87] However, since its introduction, the code has been reworked and widened in scope, based on further European legislation,[88] to become applicable to a larger amount of firms.[89] The majority of rules from the code are equal to those in the aforementioned EU legislation.[90] This and the following part will only highlight features and differences in the UK and German remuneration rules.

3.1 Limitation of remuneration

Bank employees in the areas of risk management and compliance must receive a significantly lower variable than fixed remuneration component compared to employees in other business areas.[91] This domestic UK principle may have emerged from the general CRD IV provision to maintain an appropriate balance between variable and fixed remuneration.[92] Good risk management means to compensate the

---

[83] CRR Article 450 (1)(j); CRR preamble recital (97).
[84] CRR Article 450 (2).
[85] CRR preamble recital (97).
[86] Senior management arrangements, Systems and Controls (SYSC) <https://www.the-fca.org.uk/remuneration?field_fcasf_sector=unset&field_fcasf_page_category=141> accessed 11 May 2016.
[87] Rice and Johnston (n 2) 1.
[88] Regulation (EU) No 575/2013 of 26 June 2013 on prudential requirements for credit institutions and investment firms and amending Regulation (EU) No 648/2012 OJ L176/1; Directive 2011/61/EU of 8 June 2011 on Alternative Investment Fund Managers and amending Directives 2003/41/EC and 2009/65/EC and Regulations (EC) No 1060/2009 and (EU) No 1095/2010 OJ L 174/1; Directive 2009/138/EC of 25 November 2009 on the taking-up and pursuit of the business of Insurances and Reinsurance (Solvency II) OJ L 335/1.
[89] Rice and Johnston (n 2) 1.
[90] Vide supra 4; SYSC 19D.1.6 G (2).
[91] SYSC 19D.3.18 G (3).
[92] See CRD IV Article 93 (f).

ability to maintain high profits while avoiding large losses.[93] Banks shall ensure to attract and keep experienced employees appropriately trained to fulfil their tasks, even though the variable remuneration of employees in compliance and risk management must be significantly lower than the fixed component.[94] This is controversial, as in risk management and compliance, senior highly skilled staff is needed. Such staff may have a higher incentive to perform well through variable remuneration. If risk management is measured by performing well through a minimum of losses and optimal profits,[95] only a variable component of remuneration may support such goal.

3.2 Guaranteed variable remuneration

Under the EU Directive, guaranteed variable remuneration does not promote "sound risk management" and shall only be paid in exceptional circumstances,[96] such as the employment of new staff and only during the first year, if the bank is financially stable.[97] However, the FCA takes a different approach and permits guaranteed variable remuneration if two conditions are met,[98] (1) an employee's variable component of remuneration amounts less than 33 per cent of his total remuneration,[99] and (2) the employee's total remuneration is below GBP500,000.[100] If both conditions are met, guaranteed variable remuneration may be paid in any circumstances, not only for recruitment. This derogation may create new risks for the stability of the financial market. Employees in their supervisory function for risk management may be well remunerated in fixed components only. Such employees can be influenced in their risk assessment through added guaranteed variable remuneration, which eventually could enable the whole risk management system in a bank. The general principle, to remunerate in consistence with "effective risk management",[101] may be circumvented by declaring the guaranteed variable

---

[93] E D Solozhentsev, *Risk Management Technologies: With Logic and Probabilistic Models (Topics in Safety, Risk, Reliability and Quality)* (Springer Verlag 2014) 180; Paul Sweeting, *Financial Enterprise Risk Management (Internal Series on Actuarial Science)* (CUP 2011) 510.
[94] SYSC 19D.3.18 G (3).
[95] Solozhentsev (n 93) 180; Sweeting (n 93) 510.
[96] CRD IV Article 94 (1)(d), 19D.3.44 R.
[97] CRD IV Article 94 (e).
[98] SYSC 19D.3.35 G (2)(a).
[99] SYSC 19D.3.35 G (1)(a).
[100] SYSC 19D.3.35 G (1)(b).
[101] SYSC 19D.3.36 R.

remuneration to be paid based on other performance criteria, given that the employee is influenced in his risk assessment function. Finally, this domestic provision leads to the evasion of CRD IVs restorations, with negative effects on risk control.

3.3 Remuneration committee

Banks are provided with the flexibility to set up a remuneration system appropriate for their size and complexity of activities.[102] Different banks may have to comply with the code in different ways. A larger bank with affluent or complex transactions cannot choose,[103] but must create a remuneration committee ("the committee").[104] However, smaller entities do not necessarily have to establish such a committee.[105] A bank is considered to be small if its 'management responsibilities map [is] no more than a single sheet of paper'.[106] A "single sheet of paper" does not mean a single document,[107] but may be a 'folder (…) with several files or items in it'.[108] This definition is inadequate and leaves room for determining whether or not a remuneration committee has to be established. However, it is likely that a bank is considered to be small if its gross total assets over a rolling period of five years are GBP250 million or less,[109] its business lines are narrow,[110] and 'does not rely on group governance arrangements'.[111] This gives smaller banks more freedom and protects them from extra administrative costs accompanying with a remuneration committee.

---

[102] SYSC 19D.2.2 G (1).
[103] Different to CRD IV Article 95 (1); Commission (n 9) preamble recital (2); Commission (1) recital (4).
[104] SYSC 19D.3.12 R (1).
[105] SYSC 19D.2.2 G (2).
[106] SYSC 4.5.13 G (1).
[107] SYSC 4.5.13 G (2).
[108] SYSC 4.5.13 G (3).
[109] SYSC 4.5.13 G (2)(a)(i); PRA, 'Strengthening individual accountability in banking and insurance – responses to CP14/14 and CP26/14' (Policy Statement PS 3/15, PRA 2015) <http://www.bankofengland.co.uk/pra/documents/publications/ps/2015/ps315.pdf> accessed 11 May 2016, 5, 2.14.
[110] SYSC 4.5.13 G (2)(b).
[111] SYSC 4.5.13 G (2)(c).

The committee shall be "competent and independent".[112] Therefore, only non-executive members of the management body shall be part of the committee.[113] However, in a small bank, it may be proportionate if the governing body acts as the committee.[114] This derogation may be justified due to the fact that smaller banks are less susceptible for excessive remuneration. The stability of the financial system may not be at stake,[115] because of the little importance of 'managing risk, capital and liquidity' in such banks.[116] However, financial institutions shall avoid "conflicts of interests".[117] It is controversial for a smaller bank's management to determine its own remuneration. Inappropriately designed remuneration can lead to excessive risk-taking.[118] Such does not jeopardise the stability of the financial system as a whole, but may have material effects for a Member State's economy, banks' shareholder and customers.

4. Legislation in Germany

The *Aktiengesetz* regulates the German *Aktiengesellschaft*,[119] which is the equivalent to the English Plc, a corporate form often chosen by banks.[120] The German Corporate Governance Codex ("the codex")[121] is a non-binding soft-law, and further specifies widely formulated provisions of the *Aktiengesetz*.[122] The *Kreditwesengesetz*

---

[112] SYSC 19D.3.12 R (1).
[113] CRD IV Article 95 (2); SYSC 19D.3.12 R (2)(b).
[114] SYSC 19D.2.2 G (2).
[115] CRD IV preamble recital (67); EBA (n 5) ch I, para 7.
[116] SYSC 19D.3.12 R (2)(a).
[117] CRD IV Article 88 (1) and 92 (2)(b); SYSC 19D.2.2 G(4)(c) and 19D.3.9 R; para 4.3.3 DCGK.
[118] EBA (n 5) ch I, para 3; CRD IV preamble recital (51); Röttgen and Kluge (n 5) 900; Commission (n 1) recital (2).
[119] Aktiengesetz (AktG) vom 6 September 1965 (BGBl. I S. 1089), das zuletzt durch den Artikel 1 des Gesetzes vom 22 Dezember 2015 (BGBl I S 2565) geändert worden ist <https://www.gesetze-im-internet.de/aktg/index.html> accessed 11 May 2016 (Statute regulating the German equivalent tot he English Plc).
[120] "Deutsche Bank Aktiengesellschaft (AG)" <https://www.deutsche-bank.de/pfb/content/pk-rechtliche-hinweise.html?pfb_toggle=34735-34741> accessed 11 May 2016; "Commerzbank Aktiengesellschaft" <https://www.commerzbank.de/portal/de/footer1/impressum/impressum_1.html> accessed 11 May 2016; „DZ Bank AG" <https://www.dzbank.de/content/dzbank_de/de/footermetanavigation/footerlinks/impressum.html> accessed 11 May 2016.
[121] Deutscher Corporate Governance Kodex (DCGK) (in der Fassung vom 5 Mai 2015 mit Beschlüssen aus der Plenarsitzung vom 5 Mai 2015).
[122] preamble 2 DCGK.

regulates banks.[123] The code, *Kreditwesengesetz* and the *Aktiengesetz* regulate remuneration in listed companies, such as banks.

Different from the Plc, the German *Aktiengesellschaft* has a dualistic corporate governance model. The management board runs the companies' operational business.[124] The supervisory board appoints,[125] oversees,[126] and advises the management board.[127] It is also involved in some management board's decisions.[128] The supervisory board is appointed by shareholders during the shareholder meeting.[129] For larger companies,[130] such as banks, up to 50 per cent of the supervisory board members have to be employee representatives.[131] The supervisory board shall have the same function as the remuneration committee in other countries.[132]

The banks managers' total remuneration is determined by the supervisory board,[133] and shall be proportionate to their tasks and performance.[134] The supervisory board, therefore, has latitude in determining the management's remuneration structure.[135] Furthermore, the total remuneration shall take into account the banks' overall performance and shall not exceed the "usual pay".[136] Banks listed on a regulated market shall have a sustainable remuneration structure,[137] which is the case if the

---

[123] Kreditwesengesetz in der Fassung der Bekanntmachung vom 9 September 1998 (BGBl I S 2776), das durch Artikel 4 des Gesetzes vom 11 April 2016 (BGBl I S 720) geändert worden ist („KWG).
[124] § 76 Abs 1 AktG; para 4.1.1 DCGK.
[125] § 84 Abs 1 AktG.
[126] § 111 Abs 1 AktG.
[127] para 3.2, 3.5 and 5.1.1 and 5.1.2 DCGK.
[128] § 111 Abs 4 AktG; para 3.3 and 3.9 DCGK.
[129] § 101 Abs 1 AktG.
[130] More than 500 employees, Drittelbeteiligungsgesetz (DrittelbG)vom 18 Mai 2004 (BGBl I S 974), das zuletzt durch Arkitel 8 des Gesetzes vom April 2015 (BGBl I S 642) geändert worden ist, § 1 Abs 1 Nr 1 DrittelbG; More than 2000 employees, Mitbestimmungsgesetz (MitbestG) vom 4 Mai 1976 (BGBl I S 1153), das zuletzt durch Artikel 7 des Gesetzes vom 24 April 2015 (BGBl I S 642) geändert worden ist, § 1 Abs 1 MitbestG.
[131] ⅓, § 4 Abs 1 DrittelbG; ½, § 7 Abs 1 and 2 MitbestG.
[132] Para 5.3.2 DCGK.
[133] Supervisory board (Aufsichtsrat) § 95 ff AktG); para 4.2.2 DCGK.
[134] § 87 Abs 1 S 1 AktG; para 4.2.2 second paragraph DCGK.
[135] Röttgen and Kluge (n 5) 900, 905.
[136] § 87 Abs 1 S 1 AktG; para 4.2.2 second paragraph DCGK.
[137] § 87 Abs 1 S 2 AktG.

13

variable component of remuneration takes into account a period of several years.[138] This long-term perspective is based on financial criteria only, excluding non-financial factors.[139] The supervisory board shall have the means to limit the variable remuneration in case the banks' situation declines.[140] Unlike in the UK,[141] it is not possible for the management in smaller German banks to determine its own remuneration.[142] Again, different from the UK, where the remuneration of banks in sensitive risk functions should be "significantly lower" compared to other positions,[143] the remuneration in Germany must not exceed the "usual pay". The German legislation is less strict, as it is unclear what the "usual pay" specifically is.

4.1 Limitation of remuneration

4.1.1 Total remuneration limitation

The ratio between fixed and variable remuneration in Germany is limited as in other Member States based on the CRD IV.[144] There is no national provision to limit the remuneration further to a total amount payable. However, some companies set a general cap on manager's remuneration,[145] e. g. limiting it to twenty times of the average employees pay.[146] Such a cap is not limiting the variable component,[147] but the total remuneration. The lower pay may be unappealing for a successful manager,

---

[138] § 87 Abs 1 S 3 1 Hs AktG; Christoph H Seibt, '§87' in Marcus Lutter and Karsten Schmidt (eds) Aktiengesetz Kommentar (3rd ed, Otto Schmidt Verlag 2015) § 87 para 12; Hans-Christoph Ihrig, Andre P H Wandt and Jonas Wittgens, 'Die angemessene Vorstandsvergütung drei Jahre nach Inkrafttreten des VostAG' [2012] ZIP Beilage zu Heft 2040, 1, 8; Reinhard March-Barner, 'Zum Begriff der Nachhaltigkeit in § 87 Abs. 1 AktG' [2011] ZHR 175, 737, 745; Wilsing and Paul (n 12) 363; Georg Annuß and Ingo Theusinger, 'Das VorstAG – Praktische Hinweise zum Umgang mit dem neuen Recht' [2009] BB 2434, 2435.

[139] Simone Wasserer, 'Neue Grundsätze für eine angemessene Vergütungspolitik – Zur Umsetzung der Vergütungsempfehlung der Europäischen Kommission im Rechtsvergleich Österreich und Deutschland' in Holger Altmeppen, Hanns Fitz and Heinrich Honsell, *Festschrift für Günter H. Roth zum 70. Geburtstag* (C H Beck Verlag 2011) 871; Clemens Hasenauer and Lorenz Pracht, 'Revision des Österreichischen Corporate Governance Kodex' [2010] Aufsichtsrat aktuell 1, 14.

[140] § 87 Abs 1 S 3 2 Hs, Abs 2 S 1 AktG; Deilmann and Otte (n 5) 262.

[141] SYSC 19D.2.2 G (2).

[142] § 87 Abs 1 S 1 AktG; para 4.2.2 second paragraph DCGK.

[143] SYSC 19D.3.18 G (3).

[144] § 25 a Abs 5 S 2 ff KWG.

[145] Eg "SolarWorld AG" <http://www.solarworld.de/konzern/investor-relations/corporate-governance/verguetungsbericht/> accessed 11 May 2016; Martin Murphy, 'Frank Asbeck: Eine Nummer kleiner' (Handelsblatt online, 20 Mai 2009) <http://www.handelsblatt.com/unternehmen/management/deckelung-der-vorstandsgehaelter-frank-asbeck-eine-nummer-kleiner/3180616.html> accessed 11 May 2016; Eberhard Vetter, 'Begrenzung der Vorstandsbezüge durch Hauptversammlungsbeschluss?' [2009] ZIP 1307.

[146] Eberhard Vetter, 'Begrenzung der Vorstandsbezüge durch Hauptversammlungsbeschluss?' [2009] ZIP 1307.

[147] CRD IV Article 94 (1)(g)(i) and (ii); in the UK: SYSC 19D.1.3 R (2) and 19D.3.48 R (3).

which may seek employment with a competitor. However, the implementation and supervision of such a cap are fairly easy. Furthermore, it is difficult to circumvent a general cap. If a manager wants to raise his own remuneration, he has to increase the bank employee's remuneration first. That may lead to long-term thinking in his own remuneration, also taking into account "soft criteria".[148]

4.1.2 Sustainability in listed companies

The remuneration is limited to a sustainable development of the company.[149] Variable pay is, therefore, undue if it is not based on sustainable elements.[150] The remuneration policy shall be based on a sustainable development of the company and is applicable to listed *Aktiengesellschaften* only,[151] to exclude other German corporate forms.[152] During the legislative process, it was discussed whether or not the sustainability element shall be applicable for non-listed companies.[153] The German parliament decided to exclude such entities, but make it a voluntary provision for non-listed companies.[154] Voluntary rules are unlikely to be followed, which limits the scope of the regulation on bankers pays in Germany. Moreover, listed companies may have a disadvantage as they have to follow stricter rules. Well trained staff could prefer non-listed companies as a prospective employer.

It is not clear how to interpret sustainability in the context of remuneration.[155] It can be connected to long-term ecological and social criteria.[156] Sustainability can also focus only on the time period during which the remuneration is paid. The fixed component of remuneration can be classified as a long-term instrument, regardless

---

[148] Hans-Christoph Ihrig and Carsten Schäfer, *Rechte und Pflichten des Vorstands* (Dr. Otto Schmidt Verlag 2014) 98.
[149] § 87 Abs 1 S 2 AktG; Röttgen and Kluge (n 5) 900.
[150] § 87 Abs 1 S 2 AktG; Deilmann and Otte (n 5) 262.
[151] § 87 Abs 1 S 2 AktG; preamble 1 and 2 DCGK.
[152] Deutscher Bundestag, BT-Drs 16-13433, 10; Deilmann and Otte (n 5) 261.
[153] Barbara Dauner-Lieb '§ 87'in Martin Henssler and Lutz Strohn (eds), *Gesellschaftsrecht* (2nd edn, C H Beck 2014) § 87 para 24; Deutscher Bundestag, BT-Drs 16-13433, 10; Handelsrechtsausschuss des Deutschen Anwaltsvereins, 'Stellungnahme zum Entwurf eines Gesetzes zur Angemessenheit der Vorstandsvergütung (VostAG)' [2009] NZG 612, 613.
[154] Deutscher Bundestag, BT-Drs 16-13433, 10.
[155] Röttgen and Kluge (n 5) 900.
[156] Dietmar Hexel, '10 Jahre Corporate Governance in Deutschland: Eine Bestandsaufnahme aus gewerkschaftlicher Sicht' [2012] AuR 334, 335; Wilsing and Paul (n 12) 363, 364.

how it is paid. Therefore, the total remuneration shall be composed of a third,[157] or a half,[158] or the entire fixed pay.[159] However, the statutory provision clearly states, remuneration shall consist of both, fixed and variable components.[160] Moreover, performance-oriented pay is a sufficient mean for employment motivation. The variable component shall be based on criteria, deliberating a timeframe over three to four years.[161] If so, the variable remuneration can be considered to be long-term oriented.[162]

4.2 Report

The total remuneration of every member of the management board must be published regardless the amount, divided in fixed and variable remuneration, unless the shareholders vote in extraordinary resolution against the publication.[163] EU legislation imposes the publication of total remuneration for every bank's employee if they received more than EUR one million,[164] which seems to be utterly high. Employees may tend to take higher risks at lower salary levels. The German provision is stricter but may result in higher security through "public control". The following paragraph will consider upcoming developments.

5. Future developments

A newly adopted proposal by the EU Parliament seeks to improve the financial and non-financial performance in a bank, by not only focusing on long-term factors but also the '(...) involvement of all stakeholders, particularly, employees, local

---

[157] Deilmann and Otte (n 5) 261.
[158] Julia Löhr, 'Der entzauberte MBA' *Frankfurter Allgemeine* (Frankfurt, 27 July 2009) 10.
[159] Fleischer (n 12) 803; Thüsing (n 13) 519.
[160] § 87 Abs 1 AktG; para 4.2.3 DCGK.
[161] § 87 Abs 1 S 3 AktG; Uwe Hüffer and Jens Koch, *Aktiengesetz: AktG* (12th edn, C H Beck Verlag 2016) § 87 para 4 d; Gerald Spindler, 'Vorstandsgehälter auf dem Prüfstand – das Gesetz zur Angemessenheit der Vorstandsvergütung (VostAG)' [2009] NJOZ 3282, 3285; Fleischer (n 12) 803.
[162] Patrick Velte, "Nachhaltige" Vorstandsvergütung bei börsennotierten Aktiengesellschaften: Notwendige Einbeziehung von nichtfinanziellen Leistungsindikatoren?' [2016] NZG 294, 296.
[163] Para 4.2.4 DCGK.
[164] CRD Article 73 (3).

authorities, and civil society'.[165] The remuneration shall also be based on non-financial aspects.[166] Such "soft criteria",[167] representing a "three-pillar concept",[168] focus on economic, social and ecological aspects.[169] Furthermore, non-monetary criteria shall consider '(…) pay and employment conditions of employees of the company (…)'.[170] Supervision is carried out by the shareholder meeting, which shall approve company's remuneration structure every three years.[171] Surprisingly, the UK propelled that "say on pay" policy for the EU,[172] regardless the possible effects on its financial industry. The German and American legislators refused to take non-financial

---

[165] European Parliament, Long-term shareholder engagement and corporate governance statement ***I: Amendments adopted by the European Parliament on 8 July 2015 on the proposal for a directive of the European Parliament and of the Council amending Directive 2007/36/EC as regards the encouragement of long-tersm shareholder engagement and Directive 2013/34/EU as regards certain elements of the corporate governance statement (COM(2014)0213 – C/-0147/2014 – 2014/0121(COD)) (Ordinary legislative procedure: first reading) <http://www.europarl.europa.eu/sides/getDoc.do?pubRef=-//EP//NONSGML+TA+P8-TA-2015-0257+0+DOC+PDF+V0//EN> accessed 11 May 2016, para (2a).

[166] Andre Depping and Daniel Walden, *CSR und Recht: Juristische Aspekte nachhaltiger Unternehmensfürhung erkennen und verstehen (Management-Reihe Corporate Social Respnsibility)* (Springer Gabler Verlag 2015) 88; Röttgen and Kluge (n 5) 900, 903; Wilsing and Paul (n 12) 364; Dudo von Eckardstein and Stefan Konlechner, *Vorstandsvergütung und gesellschaftliche Verantwortung der Unternehmnung: Zur Berücksichtigung der Gesellschaftlichen Funktion großer Kapitalunternehmen in Vergütungssystemen für die Mitglieder von Vorständen* (Rainer Hampp Verlag 2008) 6; Dietmar Hexel, 'Bausteine für eine angemessene Vorstandsvergütung' [2008] Der Aufsichtsrat, 128; R Edward Freeman and S Ramakrishna Valamuri, 'A new approach to CSR: Company Stakeholder Responsibility' in Andrew Kakabadse and Mette Morsing (eds), *Corporate Social Responsibility: Reconciling Aspiration with Application* (Palgrave Macmillan 2006) 86.

[167] Ihrig and Schäfer (n 148) 98.

[168] Velte (n 162) 295.

[169] Stefan Muller, Martin Stawinoga and Patrick Velte, 'Nationale Umsetzung der Mitgliedsstaatenwahlrechte der europäischen CSR-Richtlinie beim Ausweis und bei der Prüfung der „nichtfinanziellen Erklärung" [2015] ZfU 3, 313; Stefan Müller and Patrick Velte, 'Mögliche Einbettung der neuen nichtfinanziellen Erklärung in die handelsrechtliche Unternehmenspublizität und –prüfung' [2015] DB 2217; Stefan Muller, Martin Stawinoga and Patrick Velte, 'Stakeholder Expectations on CSR Management and Current Regulatory Developments in Europe and Germany' [2015] Corporate Ownership and Control 4, 505; European Parliament (n 165) para (11) and (15); Ihrig and Schäfer (n 148) 91; Röttgen and Kluge (n 5) 900, 901; Barbara Dauner-Lieb, Alexander von Preen and Stefan Simon, 'Das VostAG – Ein Schritt auf dem Weg zum Board-System?' [2010] DB 377, 379; Wilsing and Paul (n 12) 364; Anthony Ian Ogus, *Regulation: legal form and economic theory* (Clarendon 1994) 57.

[170] European Parliament (n 165) article 9 a (3) second paragraph; Dietmar Hexel, '10 Jahre Corporate Governance in Deutschland: Eine Bestandsaufnahme aus gewerkschaftlicher Sicht' [2012] AuR 334, 335.

[171] European Parliament (n 165) article 9 a (1); based on   Commission (n 9) preamble recital (10).

[172] Christoph H Seibt, 'Richtlinienvorschlag zur Weiterentwicklung des europäischen Corporate Governance-Rahmens' [2014] DB 1910, 1911.

criteria into account for long-term remuneration,[173] even though such factors could enhance sustainable stakeholder management.[174]

---

[173] Patrick Velte, '"Nachhaltige" Vorstandsvergütung bei börsennotierten Aktiengesellschaften: Notwendige Einbeziehung von nichtfinanziellen Leistungsindikatoren?' [2016] NZG 294, 296; Wasserer (n 139) 871; Hasenauer and Pracht (n 139) 14; Georg Thüsing and Gerrit Foster, 'Nachhaltigkeit als Zielvorgabe für die Vorstandsvergütung' [2010] GWR 515; Lucian A Bebchuk and Jesse M Fried, 'How to tie equity compensation to long-term results' [2010] Journal of Applied Corporate Finance Volume 22 Number 1, 99; Lucian A Bebchuk and Jesse M Fried, 'Paying for long-term performance' [2010] University of Pennsylvania Law Review Vol 158 No 7, 1915.
[174] Velte (n 162) 297.

III. Negative Impact of Regulation

1. Costs

Regulation of banker's remuneration may increase costs as the rules have to be implemented in banks, executed and a supervisory body has to be created. For the implementation, new staff has to be hired or existing employees need training. External advice may be necessary. The new remuneration policy needs to be designed or changed.[175] To manage risks associated with remuneration adequately, banks may need to purchase special risk management software's.[176] However, such software's and other necessary measures are costly, and may be an obstacle for smaller banks.[177] Supervision, secured through externals and a permanent internal supervisory body,[178] creates higher costs for banks and the public. Finally, banks have to communicate with regulatory authorities and provide data. Such (public)[179] disclosure can lead to competitive disadvantages. Those interventions will raise labour and administrative costs,[180] which finally have to be paid from banks customers, merely the public.

2. Attractiveness of the market

Europe's financial centres could become less attractive due to the regulation of remuneration. Regulation of banker's remuneration is '(...) restricting the exercise of market power in many instances'.[181] Regulation can cause competitive disadvantages for banks. Bonuses set incentives for employees' good performance and are a part of cost flexibility in a bank.[182] If an institution can only pay lower salaries, highly skilled staff may opt for another company with '(...) more attractive

---

[175] Vide supra 4.
[176] Solozhentsev (n 93) 180.
[177] ibid.
[178] Vide supra 8.
[179] As in Germany, vide supra 19.
[180] Anthony Ian Ogus, *Regulation: legal form and economic theory* (Clarendon 1994) 55.
[181] Dragomir (n 4) 41.
[182] EBA (n 5) ch I, para 37.

remuneration packages for skilled people (...)' in a financial market outside Europe.[183]

3. Common goods

Common goods can be diversely defined,[184] due to different cultural perspectives.[185] Common goods are beneficial values for the entire public or some social groups.[186] Banks have an important role in the monetary policy,[187] creating a payment system and providing loans.[188] They offer bank accounts, which are necessary for our today's financial system. Furthermore, banks gather money and redistribute liquidity to other market-participants.[189] Considering those facts, banks are of "specific public interest".[190] However, such interest is not necessarily a public good or needs special regulatory attention. Bank accounts and loans are not of more importance than any other services offered in the market. There are no apparent criteria to determine public goods.[191] Banks are private entities with rights to entrepreneurial freedom.[192] Such freedom is a fundamental right,[193] of high value for economies and should not

---

[183] David T Llewellyn, 'Institutional structure of financial regulation and supervision: The basic issues' [2006] Paper presented at a World Bank seminar Aligning Supervisory Structures with Country Needs Washington DC 6th and 7th June 2006, 8 <http://siteresources.worldbank.org/INTTOPCONF6/Resources/2057292-1162909660809/F2FlemmingLlewellyn.pdf> accessed 11 May 2016.

[184] Henri-Claude de Bettignies and Francois Lepineux, Business, *Globalization and the Common Good* (Peter Lang Verlag 2009) 254.

[185] Kadri Simm, 'The concepts of common good and public interest: From plato to Biobanking' [2011] Cambridge Quarterly of Healthcare Ethics, 554, 555; Manuel G Valasquez, *Business Ethics: Concepts and Cases* (3rd edn, Englewood Cliffs 1992) 30.

[186] Bettina Limpert, '§ 62 Auflösung durch eine Verwaltungsbehörde' in Holger Fleischer and Wulf Goette (eds), *Münchener Kommentar zum Gesetz betreffend die Gesellschaft mit beschränkter Haftung (GmbHG)* (2nd edn, CH Beck Verlag 2016) § 62 para 32; Ulrich Haas, '§ 62 Auflösung durch eine Verwaltungsbehörde' in Adolf Baumbach and Alfred Hueck (eds), *Gesetz betreffend die Gesellschaften mit beschränkter Haftung (GmbHG)* (20th edn, C H Beck Verlag 2013) § 62 para 9; Simm (n 185) 555; Anthony Ian Ogus, *Regulation: legal form and economic theory* (Clarendon 1994) 33.

[187] Dragomir (n 4) 27.

[188] Tommaso Padoa-Schioppa, *Regulating Finance: Balancing Freedom and Risk* (OUP 2004) 13 and 46.

[189] M L Burstein, 'Beyond the Banking Principle' in M L Burstein, Studies in Banking Theory, Financial History and Vertical Control (Palgrave Macmillan 1988) 63.

[190] Dragomir (n 4) 27.

[191] Limpert (n 186) § 62 para 32; Dragomir (n 4) 49; Jörg Nerlich, '§ 62 Auflösung durch eine Verwaltungsbehörde' in Lutz Michalski (ed), *Kommentar zum Gesetz betreffend die Gesellschaften mit beschränkter Haftung (GmbHG) II* (2nd edn, C H Beck 2010) § 62 para 8.

[192] Dragomir (n 4) 40.

[193] Article 16 Charter of Fundamental Rights of the European Union [2000] OJ C 364/1; Article 12 Abs 1 GG (German constitution).

be subject to any limitations. Regulations with regard to remuneration restrict such freedom.

However, if bank services are considered to be a public good, laws do not protect such good for the public. The regulations do not often promote the public good, but incentives of some individuals in a certain area.[194] It is necessary to have well-trained staff to keep and protect that good. However failure of a few banks leads to the urge of society in having someone accountable.[195] Politicians in their endless efforts to raise more votes use the public interest for their own benefit, by making the whole banking sector responsible for the action of a few. The political approach was to convince voters with stricter regulations on banks.[196] The public interest is an attractive mean to justify regulatory intervention.[197] However, the real incentive behind such action, in this case to raise votes, remains in the dark.

Limitation of remuneration to secure the public interest is not a sufficient mean to prevent market failure.[198] Conversely, over-regulating leads to a bank's business failure, which destabilises the market. Regulations may raise the risk of market failure. Moreover, the rules concerning remuneration did not really change the public opinion that managers get paid inappropriately.[199] Over-regulating should, therefore, be avoided as it does not stabilise the financial market nor satisfy the public's opinion.

---

[194] Dragomir (n 4) 49.
[195] "Lehman Brothers"; Antony Hainsworth, 'Book Review: The regulatory aftermath of the global financial crisis' [2013] 5 JBFL 307; Sachverständigenrat, *Die Zukunft nicht aufs Spiel setzen: Jahresgutachten 2009/2010* (Bonifatius GmbH Buch-Druck-Verlag 2010) 29 para 25; Benedikt Wolfers and Thomas Voland, 'Sanierung und Insolvenz von Banken unter besonderer Berücksichtigung der Vorgaben des Verfassungs- und Europarechts' in in Klaus J Hopt and Gottfried Wohlmannstetter (eds), *Handbuch Corporate Governance von Banken* (Verlag Franz Vahlen 2011) 315, 327; Thüsing and Foster (n 173) 515; Lastra and Wood (n 4) 539; Philip R Wood, 'Legal impact of the financial crisis' [2008] 11 JIBFL 575.
[196] EBA (n 5) ch I, para 3; CRD IV preamble recital (51); Röttgen and Kluge (n 5) 900; Dragomir (n 4) 19; Deilmann and Otte (n 5) 261.
[197] Dragomir (n 4) 49 and 50.
[198] Anthony Ian Ogus, *Regulation: legal form and economic theory* (Clarendon 1994) 55.
[199] Wilsing and Paul (n 12) 364.

IV. Necessity to regulate

There are three main objectives behind regulating the financial system: maintain the safety and soundness of the market, sustain systemic stability, and protect consumers.[200] Safety and soundness include the prevention excessive risk and opacity.[201] Under the public interest approach, it is necessary to regulate banks for the interest of depositors and investors.[202] Common goods are strongly connected to the public interests.[203] A stable and sound functioning banking system is beneficial for the public and therefore a public good.[204] To achieve that goal, states have to intervene by reducing '(...) the risk of bank failure and insolvency'.[205]

1. Risk exposure

Risk management is essential to keep the financial system stable and sound. Such goal may only be achieved through (further) regulations. In the past, remuneration practices encouraged bankers to take higher risks by generating short-term profits in order to raise their own variable remuneration.[206] However, such practices exposed banks to high potential losses in the long-run.[207] Without regulation, risk management control systems of banks are not sufficiently effective and strong to monitor the risk-taking at an acceptable level.[208] Those and the increasing complexity of risks led to

---

[200] Dragomir (n 4) 48; David T Llewellyn, *The Economic Rationale for Financial Regulation* (FSA Occasional Papers in Financial Regulation 1999) 9.
[201] Dragomir (n 4) 48.
[202] Dragomir (n 4) 48.
[203] Simm (n 185) 555; Clarke E Cochran, 'Political Science and "The Public Interest"' [1974] The Journal of Politics 36, 327, 328.
[204] Marie-Anne Frison-Roche, 'La prise en charge par le droit des systèmes à risques' [2000] <http://mafr.fr/media/attachments/2012/1/4/61-_droit_des_systemes_a_risques.pdf> accessed 11 May 2016, 259.
[205] Dragomir (n 4) 49.
[206] EBA (n 5) ch I, para 3; CRD IV preamble recital (51); Röttgen and Kluge (n 5) 900; Commission (n 1) preamble recital (1) - (3); Deilmann and Otte (n 5) 261.
[207] Commission (n 1) preamble recital (3).
[208] Commission (n 1) preamble recital (4).

the financial crisis.[209] It is necessary to regulate remuneration policies by reducing the burden on risk management,[210] to enable more effective systems.[211]

1.1 Remuneration

The remuneration policy in a bank shall be linked to its complexity of activities,[212] risk-focused, and not encourage excessive risk taking.[213] In many companies in the financial services industry, remuneration practices were counterproductive to solid and effective risk management.[214] Sound remuneration should consist of different instruments, which combine short- and long-term incentives.[215] A solid remuneration structure can reduce risks emanating by a bank.[216] Regulations and the ratio of fixed to variable pay leads to higher fixed remuneration components.[217] The fixed remuneration can be considered to be long-term oriented,[218] which therefore promotes sounder risk management.

1.1.1 Variable remuneration

Unregulated variable remuneration can expose a bank to higher risks. Criteria for variable components of remuneration should be predetermined and measurable, and include criteria of financial and non-financial nature.[219] Remuneration structures

---

[209] EBA (n 5) ch I, para 3; CRD IV preamble recital (51); Röttgen and Kluge (n 5) 900; Otmar Issing and Marcel Bluhm, 'Anforderungen an eine neue Ordnung der Finazmärkte' in Klaus J Hopt and Gottfried Wohlmannstetter (eds), *Handbuch Corporate Governance von Banken* (Verlag Franz Vahlen 2011) 77, 88; Wolfers and Voland (n 195) 327; Commission (n 1) preamble recital (4); Deilmann and Otte (n 5) 261; Lastra and Wood (n 4) 538.
[210] Commission (n 1) preamble recital (12).
[211] ibid (5).
[212] FCA, 'General Guidance on Proportionality: The IFPRU Remuneration Code (SYSC 19A)' (FCA, 1 July 2015) 1, 1.5; Commission (n 1) preamble recital (11); also CRD IV Article 92 (2); SYSC 19D2.2 G (2).
[213] CRD IV preamble recital (62) and (65); Commission (n 1) recital (12); SYSC 19D.1.6 G (1); in the UK: SYSC 19D.3.7 R.
[214] CRD IV preamble recital (65); Commission (n 1) preamble recital (3); SYSC 19D.1.6 G (1).
[215] Deutscher Bundestag, BT-Drs 16-13433, 10; Thüsing (n 13) 520; Klaus-Stefan Hohenstatt, 'Das Gesetz zur Angemessenheit der Vorstandsvergütung' [2009] ZIP 1349, 1351; Ulrich Seibert, 'Das VostAG – Regelungen zur Angemessenheit der Vorstandsvergütungen und zum Aufsichtsrat' [2009] WM 1489; Hartmut Bauer and Stefan Arnold, 'Festsetzung und Herabsetzung der Vorstandsvergütung nach dem VorstAG' [2009] AG 717.
[216] CRD IV preamble recital (62); Commission (n 1) preamble recital (1), (2) and (12).
[217] Wilsing and Paul (n 12) 363; Deilmann and Otte (n 5) 263.
[218] Vide supra 18.
[219] CRD IV Article 94 (1)(a) and preamble recital (64); Commission (n 9) preamble recital (6).

focussing only on time units do not suffice for sustainability.[220] Non-financial criteria should be taken into account.[221] However, such are not always sufficient to meet the objective. A CFO's variable remuneration cannot be based on customer and employee satisfaction, unless there are special reasons for that.[222] Remuneration should, therefore, be designed for individual management positions.

The total variable remuneration should be limited and deferred.[223] '(...) Full bonuses should not be awarded before the risk inherent in any deal has fully run its course'.[224] Companies should be given the possibility to reclaim the paid variable remuneration, in case the data basis used to calculate the amount is proved to be manifestly misstated.[225] That can ensure long-term thinking and reduce banks' risk exposure.

To prevent a future financial crisis, a bank's remuneration policy should not give wrong incentives and be appropriately linked to the risk a member of staff takes.[226] Regulation for employees with incentives for excessive risk-taking is necessary.[227] It means to ensure that a bank's long-term interests are met while the member of staff

---

[220] Hendrik-Michael Ringleb and others, Deutscher Corporate Governance Kodex: Kommentar (5th edn, C H Beck Verlag 2013) para 722; other opinion: Hüffer and Koch (n 161) § 87 para 11; Michael Kort, '§ 87' in Klaus J Hopt and Herbert Wiedemann, Aktiengesetz: Großkommentar (4th edn, De Gruyter Verlag 2009) § 87 para 120 and 123.

[221] Philipp Evers and Mathias Sure, 'Die Berücksichtigung von Stakeholder-Belangen im Rahmen der variablen Vorstandsvergütung: Ergebnisse einer empirischen Untersuchung zu den DAX-30-Unternehmen' [2015] 205, 210; Felix Hadwiger, Katrin Schmid and Peter Wilke, 'Die Anwendung von Sozialen und Ökologischen Kriterien in der Vorstandsvergütung' [2014] Arbeitspapier, Unternehmensmitbestimmung und Unternehmenssteuerung (working paper) Vol 293, 31; Alex von Werder and Jenny Bartz, 'Corporate Governance Report 2014: Erklärung Akzeptanz des Kodex und tatsächliche Anwendung bei Vorstandsvergütung und Unabhängigkeit des Aufsichtsrats' [2014] DB 905, 913; Marc Eulerich and Patrick Velte, 'Nachhaltigkeit und Transparenz der Vorstandsvergütung: Eine empirische Untersuchung im DAX30 unter besonderer Berücksichtigung der Bemessungsgrundlage der variablen Vergütungsanteile' [2014] IZR 73, 78; Ihrig, Wandt and Wittgens (n 138) 10; Dauner-Lieb, von Preen and Simon (n 169) 379; Jens Wagner, 'Nachhaltige Unternehmensentwicklung als Ziel der Vorstandsvergütung – Eine Annäherung an den Nachhaltigkeitsbegriff in § 87 Abs. 1 AktG' [2010] AG 774, 778; Klaus-Stefan Hohenstatt and Michael Kuhnke, 'Vergütungsstruktur und variable Vergütungsmodelle für Vorstandsmitglieder nach dem VostAG' [2009] ZIP 1981, 1982; Ulrich Seibert, 'Das VostAG – Regelungen zur Angemessenheit der Vorstandsvergütungen und zum Aufsichtsrat' [2009] WM 1489, 1490.

[222] Wilsing and Paul (n 12) 364.

[223] Commission (n 1) preamble recital (14); Commission (n 9) preamble recital (6); SYSC 19D.3.59 R.

[224] Paul Sweeting, Financial Enterprise Risk Management (Internal Series on Actuarial Science) (CUP 2011) 510.

[225] Commission (n 9) preamble recital (6); Commission (n 1) preamble recital (15).

[226] EBA (n 5) ch I, para 3.

[227] Commission (n 1) preamble recital (13).

aims to reach personal objectives.[228] A maximum ratio of the variable to fixed component of remuneration 'prevents inappropriate risk taking'[229] and allows a certain degree of business freedom in determining such ratio.[230]

The regulation of remuneration policy should ensure that it is in line with the bank's business strategy and values,[231] as well as other factors apart from the financial performance, such as matters of compliance with regulation on the relationship between clients and investors or control systems within the bank.[232] Performance related to remuneration is linked to the economic environment.[233] To control risk-taking future risks should linked to performance.[234]

1.1.2 Allowances

To make sure that banks comply with the ratio limitation of variable pay, it is important to categorise remuneration correctly under the fixed or variable category.[235] Otherwise, the ratio would be of no effect. After the enforcement of CRD IV, several banks introduced "allowances", which were treated as fixed remuneration.[236] Allowances are additional payment to the existing fixed and variable remuneration.[237] The introduction of such allowances leads to a looser policy in granting variable remuneration and an increase in the total fixed remuneration.[238] Allowances can be categorised as "market value" and "role-based" allowances.[239] Banks tend to classify

---

[228] ibid (14); in the UK: SYSC 19D.3.8 R.
[229] CRD IV preamble recital (65).
[230] ibid.
[231] Commission Recommendation (2009/384/EC) of 30 April 2009 on remuneration policies in the financial services sector [2009] L 120/22 preamble recital (17).
[232] CRD IV preamble recital (63); Commission Recommendation (2009/384/EC) of 30 April 2009 on remuneration policies in the financial services sector [2009] L 120/22 preamble recital (17).
[233] EBA (n 5) ch I, para 32.
[234] CRD IV Article 94 (1)(k) and preamble recital (63).
[235] EBA (n 5) ch I, para 1.
[236] Bradley Rice, 'Allowances: Fixed or Variable Pay?' [2014] CSR 17, 136; EBA (n 5) ch I, para 5; Rice (n 12) 136.
[237] Moritz Seiler and Damian Fischer, ''Bonus Bongs' for Bankers: A New Type of Debt-Based Remunerating in the Financial Industry' [2015] ECFR 12(3), 425, 444; EBA (n 5) ch I, recital 9.
[238] EBA (n 5) ch I, para 28; Rice (n 12) 136.
[239] ibid para 13.

both types as fixed remuneration.[240] However, it is necessary to distinguish between them.[241]

"Market-value" allowances increase the basic fixed salary and are granted to members of staff which work abroad and would earn more if being remunerated in their domestic labour market.[242] Such allowances are normally predetermined and paid to all employees in a non-discriminatory way for a limited time abroad.[243] Market-value allowances can unproblematically be classified as fixed remuneration.[244]

"Role-based"[245] allowances raise the total fixed remuneration, for a limited period of time, of some predetermined member of staff in senior or executive positions.[246] Those allowances are paid on a performance basis for managers who particularly exceed the limitation of variable pay.[247] Qualifying role-based allowances as fixed remuneration leads to an increase of fixed remuneration, giving latitude to increase the total variable remuneration.[248] The EBA, different from banks, classifies most role-based allowances as typical variable remuneration.[249] Most banks would not comply with the ratio without the use of allowances.[250]

The CRD IV distinguishes only between fixed and variable remuneration,[251] there is no other classification.[252] "Role-based" allowances should be allocated to variable remuneration to promote a "sound risk management".[253] If classified as fixed remuneration, bankers may be willing to take excessive risks to maintain their

---

[240] ibid 9 and 10.
[241] ibid 13.
[242] ibid 13 (a).
[243] ibid.
[244] ibid.
[245] With a detailed list of conditions EBA (n 5) ch I, para 28 - 38.
[246] EBA (n 5) ch I, para 13 (b) and 14.
[247] ibid 13 (b) and 18.
[248] ibid para 13 (b).
[249] EBA (n 5) ch I, para 15.
[250] ibid para 20.
[251] CRD IV Article 92 (2)(g).
[252] CRD IV Article 92 (2)(g); EBA (n 5) ch I, para 22 and 24.
[253] CRD IV Article 74 (1) and 92 (2)(a); CRD IV preamble recital (64) and (65); EBA (n 5) ch I, para 23 and 35.

allowances in a downturn.²⁵⁴ In such a state, bankers could be willing to take higher risks to secure their own remuneration and thus multiply the risk exposure for the financial market as a whole.²⁵⁵

Therefore, following the CRD provisions, "role-based" allowances should be considered as variable and not fixed remuneration.²⁵⁶ Banks are expected to adjust their remuneration policy in accordance with Article 94 of the CRD IV and treat such allowances as variable remuneration.²⁵⁷ However, the legislators should further concretise the distinction between "market value" and "role-based" allowances to reduce the risk of the wrong categorisation.

1.2 Supervision

Effective risk management can only be achieved if the remuneration granting policy is transparent, avoids conflicts of interests, and ensures the independence of involved staff.²⁵⁸ Supervision ensures that those objectives are met in order to reduce a bank's risk exposure. Mandatory disclosure requirements ensure the integrity of banks and their employees.²⁵⁹ In the past, extensive public interventions were necessary to secure the European financial system,²⁶⁰ which is why banks have to be monitored to prevent from future financial crisis.²⁶¹ Supervision should, therefore, focus on the risk associated with conflicts of interests.

---

[254] EBA (n 5) ch I, para 36.
[255] CRD IV preamble recital (51).
[256] EBA (n 5) ch I, para 39.
[257] ibid para 40.
[258] DCGO 4.3.3; Commission (n 1) preamble recital (18) and (19).
[259] David T Llewellyn, 'The Institutional Structure of Regulatory Agencies' in Central Banking, *How Countries Supervise their Bank, Insurers and Securities Markets* (Central Banking Publications 1999) 11.
[260] EBA (n 5) ch I, para 3; CRD IV preamble para (51); Röttgen and Kluge (n 5) 900; Dragomir (n 4) 19; Deilmann and Otte (n 5) 261.
[261] Commission Report (n 75) 4.

1.2.1 Credit Rating

Credit ratings are means of supervising risks. Credit-rating agencies make the financial market more transparent by publishing information.[262] However, the "over-reliance" on external credit ratings should be reduced, and instead, internal ratings should be adopted by banks.[263] The market of credit rating is controlled by three undertakings[264],[265] which hold 90 per cent of the market share in Europe.[266] Such an oligopoly can increase the risk for the financial market as a whole as those institutions may be influenced by other factors, such as remuneration. The credit rating agencies offered consulting services to banks whose securities they rated or helped to design.[267] Sound ratings from external advisors can be utilised to disclose fewer banks risk than there actually are. The banks management may legally pay a rating agency to rate products created by that same credit-rating institution. The rating is very likely to be influenced by a conflict of interests.

One criterion for variable pay can be the risk management.[268] The banks' risk-takers may hire credit-rating agencies with unreliable ratings to raise their own remuneration. Therefore, banks shall ensure to conduct internal ratings, free from conflicts of interests, as well as introduce a transparent remuneration mechanism for staff involved in ratings and ensure their independence. Otherwise, if internal ratings are led by wrong financial incentives, they may lose credibility and jeopardise the stability of the financial market,[269] similar to the case of external credit ratings. The

---

[262] Dragomir (n 4) 28.
[263] CRD IV preamble recital (71); Dragomir (n 4) 19.
[264] Moodey's Investors, Standard & Poor's (S&P) and Fitch Ratings; LexisPSL 'Impact of credit ratings downgrades' [2016] LexisPSL Restructuring & Insolvency Practical Guidance <www.lexisnexis.com/uk/lexispsl/financialservices/document/393783/55MK-MBW1-F18D-T2XT> accessed 11 May 2016
[265] CRD IV preamble recital (73).
[266] ESMA, 'Competition and choice in the credit rating industry: Market share calculation required by Article 8d of Regulation 1060/2009 on Credit Rating Agencies as amended' (ESMA, 18 December 2015) <https://www.esma.europa.eu/sites/default/files/library/2015-1879_esma_cra_market_share_calculation.pdf> accessed 1 May 2016, 8 Table 2.
[267] Thomas Ross, 'The role of rating agencies and their potential exposure in the ongoing credit crisis' [2008] 7 JIBFL 349, 351; Konrad-Adenauer-Stiftung, 'Welche Rolle spielten die Ratingagenturen bei der Entstehung der Finanzkriese?' (Konrad-Adenauer-Stiftung) <http://www.kas.de/wf/de/71.7074/> accessed 1 May 2016.
[268] CRD IV Article 94 (1)(j) and (k); in the UK: SYSC 19D.3.23 R.
[269] CRD IV preamble recital (51).

latter may be used as one out of several factors in the process to determine risk, but not solely.[270]

1.2.2 Internal supervision

Supervision should be carried out in several stages. External supervision through authorities is necessary to control bankers.[271] Internal supervision of risk management should be a mandatory requirement to assist the external supervision and minimise the avoidance of existing regulations. Therefore, all employees should get involved.[272] Staff responsible for risk management and supervision of risk should be separated, adopting an appropriate control system.[273] Such a mechanism should include that employee responsible for supervision change the department they monitor regularly, in order to avoid getting into conflicts of interests. The supervision of risk management leads to better performance in the area.[274] The bank's management should adopt a periodical review to ensure that the risk management is integrated into the design of remuneration policies.[275] External advisors should regularly review the system to ensure its effectiveness.[276] However, consultants may have conflicts of interests when they advise the managing board and the remuneration committee at the same time, which is why the latter should exercise caution when hiring remuneration advisors.[277] The design and implementation of a bank's remuneration policy are more effective if its stakeholders, including, where applicable, employee representatives are engaged and informed through the process. That is the reason why the relevant information should be disclosed.[278] It is necessary to make supervision mandatory by regulations.

---

[270] CRD IV preamble recital (72).
[271] Vide supra 8.
[272] Gang Chen, 'Talk about Foreign Commercial Banks Operating Risk Prevention of Reference and Enlightenment in Sweden for Example' in Jean Pierre Miahouakana Matondo and Xiaokang Zhao (eds), *2014 International Conference on Economic and Management (ICEM 2014)* (DEStech Publications Inc 2014) 311.
[273] Commission (n 1) preamble recital (4).
[274] FSB, 'Implementing the FSB principles for sound compensation practices and their implementation standards' [2015] FSB Fourth progress report, 15 <http://www.fsb.org/wp-content/uploads/FSB-Fourth-progress-report-on-compensation-practices.pdf> accessed 11 May 2016.
[275] CRD IV preamble recital (66).
[276] para 4.2.2 third paragraph DCGK; Commission (n 1) preamble recital (19).
[277] Commission (n 9) preamble recital (12).
[278] Commission (n 1) preamble recital (20).

1.2.3 High earners

Employees with '(...) material impact on (...) the [bank's] risk profile (...)'[279] and being remunerated more than EUR one million ("high earners") per fiscal year have to be publicly disclosed.[280] The high amount of that threshold can be questioned, as employees being remunerated less may also tend to take higher risk. One could argue that the overall risk may only be noteworthy for employees which remuneration exceeds the threshold. Moreover, if an employee's remuneration consists remarkably of a variable component, the threshold may not be reached due to his bad performance, which would not be publicly reported. The regulations objective would be neglected. Moreover, the threshold narrows the scope of the regulations, as there are only a few high earners in a bank. Conversely, the impact of risk from those not being high earners may be more serious, since more members of staff would be in the scope of the regulation. Reassessing the risk, the EU must have come to a similar conclusion and lowered the threshold to EUR500,000.[281]

Furthermore, the scope of the regulations has been extended. Members of staff with '(...) no material impact on the [bank's] risk profile (...)'[282] are now also being addressed. If such an employee is remunerated more than EUR750,000, a competent authority has to approve his salary up front.[283] Likewise, approval is necessary for employees with no high-risk profile, if remunerated more than EUR one million, and shall only be granted in "exceptional circumstances".[284] However, the new thresholds may still be too high for an effective risk oversight.

---

[279] Article 450 (1) CRR.
[280] Vide supra 10; Article 450 (1)(i) CRR.
[281] Parliament, Regulation of 4 March 2014 supplementing Directive 2013/36/EU of the European Parliament and of the Council with regard to regulatory technical standards with respect to qualitative and appropriate quantitative criteria to identify categories of staff whose professional activities have a material impact on an institution's risk profile [2014] OJ L 167/30, Article 4 (1)(a).
[282] ibid Article 4 (2)(b).
[283] ibid Article 5.
[284] ibid Article 5, third paragraph.

2. Stability of the Financial System

The aim of the legislations is to '(...) protect and foster financial stability (...)',[285] in the growing and globalised European banking sector.[286] Regulations of the banking sector may create trust within the monetary system. [287] Such trust will stabilise the European banking market. Investors' and depositors' confidence is one of the most important aspects of the stability of the financial system.[288] Distrust, on the other hand, may lead to massive deposit withdrawals which can result in illiquidity and bankruptcy of a financial institution.[289]

The failure of one bank may have a negative effect on other financial institutions and finally for the economy as a whole. Such a "domino effect"[290] can cause a systematic risk spreading through the market.[291] The liberality can induce systematic failure.[292] The introduction of laws regulating the mark creates new trust in the system. Trust is based on psychological factors such as stability of a financial institution and the performance of the market as a whole.[293] Therefore, scholars concluded that system relevant banks need to be protected through regulation, in order to prevent an institution's failure and regain trust in the financial market.[294]

Guaranteed financial help for failing banks is against the principle of entrepreneurial freedom.[295] One of the fundamental pillars of the market economy is to be liable for actions which lead to financial losses or insolvency.[296] However, guaranteed financial state-aid disturbs the functioning market economy.[297] Liability of banks' risks is not imposed on their shareholders, management or creditors, but the state and its tax-

---

[285] CRD IV preamble recital (51) and (67); EBA (n 5) ch I, para 7; Dragomir (n 4) 53.
[286] Dragomir (n 4) 23.
[287] Ingo Wörner, *Europäische Bankenregulierung im Spannungsverhältnis zwischen Regulierungswettbewerb und Harmonisierungsbemühungen* (Nomos Verlag 2000) 64.
[288] Dragomir (n 4) 49.
[289] Dragomir (n 4) 29.
[290] Dragomir (n 4) 30; Wolfers and Voland (n 195) 328.
[291] Padoa-Schioppa (n 188) 10.
[292] Wolfers and Voland (n 195) 327.
[293] Christoph Ohler, 'Bankensanierung als staatliche Aufgabe' [2010] WiVerw 47, 57.
[294] Gunnar Schuster, '"Too big to fail" als Rechtsproblem' [2010] Der Betrieb 71; Uwe H Scheider, 'Zwischenruf: Was ist eine systemisch relevante Bank?' [2009] ZRP 119, 120.
[295] Dragomir (n 4) 40; Issing and Bluhm (n 209) 88 Wolfers and Voland (n 195) 328.
[296] Issing and Bluhm (n 209) 88; Wolfers and Voland (n 195) 328.
[297] Issing and Bluhm (n 209) 88.

payers.[298] In conclusion, there is a "socialisation of losses".[299] Bankers have an incentive to take higher risks, due to the "public safety-net".[300] This is also called the "moral hazard problem".[301] It describes the phenomenon of being willing to take higher risks in order to maximise benefits, without being accountable for associated risks. The risk leads to a destabilised financial system, which is a potential threat to the public.[302] Banks would simply rely on government aid while taking excessive risks.[303] States have only limited means and could find themselves in financial difficulties.[304] To prevent such "moral hazard" it should be ensured that '(…) no financial firm is "too big to fail" (…)',[305] "which means a bank is so interconnected, that its insolvency could trigger the failure of the entire financial system.[306] Further regulating bankers remuneration is another way to prevent banks failure in the first place.[307]

Banks provide important services for the public.[308] The general access to banks is of public interests,[309] and the banking system itself represents a public good.[310] Public interests and public goods are often seen as identical concepts.[311] Such interests or goods may be jeopardised by excessive risk taking. Regulations of remuneration and disclosure can lead to trust, achieved by transparency. Information falls also under

---

[298] Wolfers and Voland (n 195) 328.
[299] Johann Eckenhoff, 'Finanz- und Wirtschaftskriese als Chance' [2010] KSzW 137, 138; Christoph Ohler, 'Bankensanierung als staatliche Aufgabe' [2010] WiVerw 47, 57.
[300] Dragomir (n 4) 30; Wolfers and Voland (n 195) 328.
[301] Dragomir (n 4) 30; David T Llewellyn, *The Economic Rationale for Financial Regulation* (FSA Occasional Papers in Financial Regulation 1999) 28.
[302] Wolfers and Voland (n 195) 328.
[303] Sachverständigenrat (n 195) 131 para 191.
[304] Dragomir (n 4) 40; Wolfers and Voland (n 195) 328.
[305] Dragomir (n 4) 41; Cannes Summit Final Declaration, 'Building our common future: Renewed collective action for the benefit of all' [2011] para 28 <http://www.g20.utoronto.ca/2011/2011-cannes-declaration-111104-en.html> accessed 11 May 2016; Wolfers and Voland (n 195) 329.
[306] Issing and Bluhm (n 209) 88; Wolfers and Voland (n 195) 327; Wolfgang Marotzke, 'Das deutsche Insolvenzrecht in systemischen Kriesen' [2009] JZ 763; Christoph Kaserer, Johannes Köndgen and Christoph Möllers, 'Stellungnahmen zum Finanzmarktstabilisierungsergänzungsgesetz' [2009] ZBB 142, 150; Michael Droege, 'Die wiederkehr des Staates – Eigentumsfreiheit zwischen privatem Nutzen und sozialisiertem Risiko' [2009] DVBl 1415, 1419.
[307] Wolfers and Voland (n 195) 329.
[308] Dragomir (n 4) 27; Padoa-Schioppa (n 188) 13 and 46.
[309] Dragomir (n 4) 27.
[310] Frison-Roche (n 204) 259.
[311] Simm (n 185) Alasdair MacIntyre; 'The Privatization of Good: An Inaugural Lecture' [1990] Review of Politics 344; Clarke E Cochran, 'Political Science and "The Public Interest"' [1974] The Journal of Politics 36, 327.

the category of public goods, which can be achieved through transparency and regulatory intervention.[312]

Competition is important for a stable and functioning market. However, if the state has to save a bank with public money, it may lead to the distortion of competition,[313] which can jeopardise the common good.[314] The competition among banks operating cross-border is immense. That's why it is important to ensure that all market participants follow '(...) principles on sound remuneration policy (...)'.[315] However, to be more effective, the same rules on remuneration policies should be applied in a consistent manner to all operating banks globally.[316] It is important to improve the risk management in financial institutions and adjust remuneration incentives with sustainable performance, so that the financial system is maintained stable and reliable for the future.[317] After the financial crisis, it was necessary to regain confidence among banks and in the banking industry, to restore the flow of credit for the economy and prevent further economic decrease.[318] Effective risk management may only be achieved if all market participants follow regulation in the area. If only some countries impose regulations of remuneration, banks may relocate their registered office in a country with more favourable rules. However, the risk management for the entire financial system can only be ensured when all banks apply remuneration practices in line with sustainable banking.

The regulation of bankers' remuneration is necessary to restructure the financial sector in order to achieve long-term viability and create a functioning European banking sector.[319] Finally, regulations can provide "safety-and-soundness" and

---

[312] Dragomir (n 4) 49.
[313] Wolfers and Voland (n 195) 328.
[314] Gerald Spindler, '§ 396 Voraussetzungen' in Gerald Spindler and Eberhard Stilz (eds), *Kommentar zum Aktiengesetz: AktG* (3rd edn, C H Beck Verlag 2015) § 396 para 4; Wolfgang Zöllner and Ulrich Noack, *Kölner Kommentar zum Aktiengesetz: Kölner Komm AktG Band 6: §§ 291 – 392 und §§ 15-22 AktG* (3rd edn, Carl Heymanns 2004) § 396 para 12.
[315] CRD IV Article 94 (1)(g)(iii) second paragraph; Commission (n 1) preamble recital (6).
[316] Commission (n 1) preamble recital (6).
[317] Röttgen and Kluge (n 5) 900; Commission Report (n 75) 4; Commission (n 1) preamble recital (7) and (12).
[318] Commission Report (n 75) 4.
[319] ibid.

confidence of its users, by supporting a stable financial system,[320] which is a public good and need protecting.[321]

3. Protecting the public

The public needs protecting. Bankers tend to take higher risks for their own shake, opting for higher remuneration,[322] which finally leads to higher costs for society.[323] The tax-payers have to bear the costs of failing banks,[324] which received bail-out.[325] Consumers need protecting through regulations of banks.[326] Moreover, banks are large entities with numerous employees, representing a part of the public and may lose their employment if the banks fail. Regulating the remuneration will indirectly protects consumers and employees' as banks tend to take fewer risks.[327] Regulations on bankers' remuneration can lower the risk exposure and, therefore, ensure a safe and sound functioning of the system through consumer protection and a stable financial market.[328]

---

[320] Dragomir (n 4) 41; Llewellyn (n 320) 9.
[321] Dragomir (n 4) 27.
[322] CRD IV preamble recital (62).
[323] Commission (n 1) preamble recital (1) and (2); Commission Report (n 10) 3; Commission (n 9) preamble recital (7).
[324] Cannes Summit Final Declaration (n 305) para 28.
[325] Dragomir (n 4) 19 and 20; Issing and Bluhm (n 209) 88.
[326] Dragomir (n 4) 41 and 53.
[327] Dragomir (n 4) 53.
[328] Dragomir (n 4) 54.

V. Alternative regulatory proposal

There are several alternatives to the current legislation in order to control the risks emerging from excessive remuneration. It is possible to limit the total remuneration of a banker to a factor of the common pay of an average employee in a bank.[329] Another way is adopted by Japanese banks, which do not pay based on their employees' performance but their seniority.[330] More experienced employees receive higher remuneration. The gap between the pay of management and ordinary workforce is not significantly large,[331] and there is no incentive for excessive risk taking. However, both approaches intervene with a banks freedom of business, and may lead to negative consequences for the institutions or the public financial marketplace.[332]

Alternatively, the legislators could intervene in an earlier stage, before the risks of excessive remuneration emerge. The banks risks intensive (investment)[333] business could be separated from safer commercial activities,[334] similarly to the past US Glass Segal Act.[335] Separating those business areas may be beneficial for the banks and thus, achieve the EU legislators' objectives. At first appearance, this proposal may be seen to fuel more bank regulations. However, when banks separated those business areas, the investment banking should mainly be deregulated. That statement seems to be illogical from a risk management perspective, but however it is not the case.

Different from the Glass Segal Act, a bank should not only be either way an investment or commercial banking institution. The commercial banking should stay regulated as it is, to prevent the failure of such business or ensure a publicly available and stable financial market. On the other hand, the investment banking

---

[329] Vide supra 17.
[330] BIS, 'Executive remuneration: Discussion paper' (Department for Business Innovation & Skills September 2011) 13.
[331] ibid.
[332] Vide supra 24.
[333] Investment banking.
[334] Eg providing accounts or offering loans.
[335] Julia Maues, 'Banking Act of 1933, commonly called Glass-Stegall' Federal Reserve History <http://www.federalreservehistory.org/Events/DetailView/25> accessed 11 May 2016.

should be liberalised, with only little state intervention. European banks could become more competitive to market participants in other financial jurisdictions.

However, even though a bank may still operate an investment and commercial divisions, both areas have to be separated to achieve a risk stability. There shall not be capital connections between a bank's investment and commercial business. The stability of the commercial part has to be ensured in the case of failure in the investment section. Both areas shall have different employees and different management with regard to critical areas. It is necessary to separate staff who are responsible for risk management and risk supervision.[336] This action aims to ensure that regulative requirements are fulfilled and the risk exposure of the commercial business is kept at the minimum. Moreover, investment risk-takers have to be separated from commercial bankers. The bank may share administrative tasks. That can keep costs lower than having completely independent institutions for investment and commercial banking. Stakeholders of the investment division must be enlightened over the risks of losing their investment or financial losses in case of insolvency. They have the freedom to choose with whom they want to enter business with. However, the commercial part may not take any liability for the investment banking.

This alternative proposal can ensure the safe and sound functioning of the financial market and protect relevant groups, while allowing banks to have entrepreneur freedom through a fair compromise. If the investment business fails, it can go into insolvency but stakeholders of the commercial business will not be affected.

---

[336] Commission (n 1) preamble recital (4).

VI. Conclusion

This book has shown arguments for and against bankers' remuneration regulations. Prevalent arguments consent that regulations have overall positive effects on securing the public by stabilising the European financial market.

The CRD IV aims to harmonise bankers' remuneration EU-wide. However, Member States interpreted and adopted the Directives provisions differently. The UK regulates bankers' remuneration stricter than Germany. It is a surprise as London is a better recognised financial hub than Frankfurt. However, the UK promotes small banks with less regulations and gives possible loopholes in guaranteed variable pay. Germany adopts a less strict practice, only limiting remuneration of listed banks, with the vague term of "sustainability". Disclosure requirements are stricter in Germany than in the UK. Shortly in the future, remuneration requirements will not be based on financial criteria only anymore.

Arguments against regulations of bankers' remuneration are disproved, as such intervention is necessary for states to control the risk of the market. A functioning financial system is a public good of high importance, ultimately ensuring the freedom of business. However, it is important that the terms in legislative provisions are clear. The legislators should further concretise how to categorise remuneration in fixed and variable components to avoid circumvention of the law. Furthermore, the disclosure requirements for banks should be reconsidered.

The alternative regulative proposal shows that there is not only one way to achieve the determined objectives. Other measures to control the risk, such as the proposed a strict separation in a bank's business activities, should be discussed in open academic dialogues.

Bibliography

Articles

LexisPSL,	'Impact of credit ratings downgrades' [2016] LexisPSL Restructuring & Insolvency Practical Guidance <www.lexisnexis.com/uk/lexispsl/financialservices/document/393 783/55MK-MBW1-F18D-T2XT> accessed 11 May 2016
Annuß G/ Theusinger I,	'Das VorstAG – Praktische Hinweise zum Umgang mit dem neuen Recht' [2009] BB 2434
Bauer H/ Arnold S,	'Festsetzung und Herabsetzung der Vorstandsvergütung nach dem VorstAG' [2009] AG 717
Bebchuk L A/ Fried J M,	'How to tie equity compensation to long-term results' [2010] Journal of Applied Corporate Finance Vol 22 No 1, 99
	'Paying for long-term performance' [2010] University of Pennsylvania Law Review Vol 158 No 7, 1915
Cochran C E,	'Political Science and "The Public Interest"' [1974] The Journal of Politics 36, 327
Dauner-Lieb B,	'Die Verrechtlichung der Vorstandsvergütung durch das VostAG als Herausforderung für den Aufsichtsrat – Methodische Probleme im Umgang mit Rechtsunsicherheit' [2009] Der Konzern 583
Dauner-Lieb B/ von Preen A/ Simon S,	'Das VostAG – Ein Schritt auf dem Weg zum Board-System?' [2010] DB 377
Deilmann B/ Otte S,	'Auswirkungen des VostAG auf die Struktur der Vorstandsvergütung' [2009] GWR 261
Droege M,	'Die wiederkehr des Staates – Eigentumsfreiheit zwischen privatem Nutzen und sozialisiertem Risiko' [2009] DVBl 1415
Eckenhoff J,	'Finanz- und Wirtschaftskriese als Chance' [2010] KSzW 137
Eulerich M/ Velte P,	'Nachhaltigkeit und Transparenz der Vorstandsvergütung: Eine empirische Untersuchung im DAX30 unter besonderer Berücksichtigung der Bemessungsgrundlage der variablen Vergütungsanteile' [2014] IZR 73

Evers P/ Sure M,	'Die Berücksichtigung von Stakeholder-Belangen im Rahmen der variablen Vorstandsvergütung: Ergebnisse einer empirischen Untersuchung zu den DAX-30-Unternehmen' [2015] 205
FCA,	'General Guidance on Proportionality: The IFPRU Remuneration Code (SYSC 19A)' (FCA, 1 July 2015) 1
Fleischer H,	'Das Gesetz zur Angemessenheit der Vorstandsvergütung (VostAG)' [2009] NZG 801
Frison-Roche M A,	'La prise en charge par le droit des systèmes à risques' [2000] <http://mafr.fr/media/attachments/2012/1/4/61-_droit_des_systemes_a_risques.pdf> accessed 11 May 2016, 259
Hadwiger F/ Schmid K/ Wilke P,	'Die Anwendung von Sozialen und Ökologischen Kriterien in der Vorstandsvergütung' [2014] Arbeitspapier, Unternehmensmitbestimmung und Unternehmenssteuerung (working paper) Vol 293
Hainsworth A,	'Book Review: The regulatory aftermath of the global financial crisis' [2013] 5 JBFL 307
Handelsrechtsausschuss des Deutschen Anwaltsvereins	'Stellungnahme zum Entwurf eines Gesetzes zur Angemessenheit der Vorstandsvergütung (VostAG)' [2009] NZG 612
Hasenauer C/ Pracht L,	'Revision des Österreichischen Corporate Governance Kodex' [2010] Aufsichtsrat aktuell 1
Hexel D,	'Bausteine für eine angemessene Vorstandsvergütung' [2008] Der Aufsichtsrat, 128
	'10 Jahre Corporate Governance in Deutschland: Eine Bestandsaufnahme aus gewerkschaftlicher Sicht' [2012] AuR 334
Hohenstatt K S,	'Das Gesetz zur Angemessenheit der Vorstandsvergütung' [2009] ZIP 1349
Hohenstatt K S/ Kuhnke M,	'Vergütungsstruktur und variable Vergütungsmodelle für Vorstandsmitglieder nach dem VostAG' [2009] ZIP 1981
Ihrig H C/ Wandt A P H/ Wittgens J,	'Die angemessene Vorstandsvergütung drei Jahre nach Inkrafttreten des VostAG' [2012] ZIP Beilage zu Heft 2040, 1
Kaserer C/ Köndgen J/ Möllers C,	'Stellungnahmen zum Finanzmarktstabilisierungsergänzungsgesetz' [2009] ZBB 142

Kort M,	'Vorstandshandeln im Spannungsverhältnis zwischen Unternehmensinteresse und Aktionärsinteressen' [2012] AG 605
Lastra R M/ Wood G,	'The Crisis of 2007-09: Nature, Causes and Reactions' [2010] J Int Economic Law 13 (3), 531
Llewellyn D T,	'Institutional structure of financial regulation and supervision: The basic issues' [2006] Paper presented at a World Bank seminar Aligning Supervisory Structures with Country Needs Washington DC 6th and 7th June 2006, 8 <http://siteresources.worldbank.org/INTTOPCONF6/Resources/2057292-1162909660809/F2FlemmingLlewellyn.pdf> accessed 11 May 2016
Löhr J,	'Der entzauberte MBA' *Frankfurter Allgemeine* (Frankfurt, 27 July 2009) 10
MacIntyre A,	'The Privatization of Good: An Inaugural Lecture' [1990] Review of Politics 344
Marotzke W,	'Das deutsche Insolvenzrecht in systemischen Kriesen' [2009] JZ 763
Marsch-Barner R,	'Zum Begriff der Nachhaltigkeit in § 87 Abs. 1 AktG' [2011] ZHR 175, 737
Muller S/ Stawinoga M/ Velte S,	'Stakeholder Expectations on CSR Management and Current Regulatory Developments in Europe and Germany' [2014] Corporate Ownership and Control 4/2015, 505 'Nationale Umsetzung der Mitgliedsstaatenwahlrechte der europäischen CSR-Richtlinie beim Ausweis und bei der Prüfung der „nichtfinanziellen Erklärung" [2015] ZfU 3, 313
Müller S/ Velte P,	'Mögliche Einbettung der neuen nichtfinanziellen Erklärung in die handelsrechtliche Unternehmenspublizität und –prüfung' [2015] DB 2217
Murphy, M	'Frank Asbeck: Eine Nummer kleiner' (Handelsblatt online, 20 Mai 2009) <http://www.handelsblatt.com/unternehmen/management/deckelung-der-vorstandsgehaelter-frank-asbeck-eine-nummer-kleiner/3180616.html> accessed 11 May 2016
Ohler C,	'Bankensanierung als staatliche Aufgabe' [2010] WiVerw 47

Persaud A D,	'A ticking time bomb: TLAC and other attempts to privatise bank bail-outs' [2016] 3 JIBFL 160
Rice B,	'Allowances: Fixed or Variable Pay?' [2014] 38 CSR 17, 136
Rice B/ Johnston L,	'Bankers' Bonuses Back in the Spotlight' [2014] 38 CSR 1, 1
Ross T,	'The role of rating agencies and their potential exposure in the ongoing credit crisis' [2008] 7 JIBFL 349
Röttgen N/ Kluge H G,	'Nachhaltigkeit bei Vorstandsvergütungen' [2013] NJW 900
Scheider U H,	'Zwischenruf: Was ist eine systemisch relevante Bank?' [2009] ZRP 119
Schuster G,	'"Too big to fail" als Rechtsproblem' [2010] Der Betrieb 71
Seibert U,	'Das VostAG – Regelungen zur Angemessenheit der Vorstandsvergütungen und zum Aufsichtsrat' [2009] WM 1489
	'Finanzmarktkriese, Corporate Governance, Aufsichtsrat' [2009] DB 1167
Seibt C H,	'Richtlinienvorschlag zur Weiterentwicklung des europäischen Corporate Governance-Rahmens' [2014] DB 1910
Seiler M/ Fischer D,	''Bonus Bongs' for Bankers: A New Type of Debt-Based Remunerating in the Financial Industry' [2015] ECFR 12(3), 425
Simm K,	Kadri, 'The concepts of common good and public interest: From plato to Biobanking' [2011] Cambridge Quarterly of Healthcare Ethics, 554
Spindler G,	'Vorstandsgehälter auf dem Prüfstand – das Gesetz zur Angemessenheit der Vorstandsvergütung (VostAG)' [2009] NJOZ 3282
Stech, R	'Poling the hornet's nest: an analysis of EU proposals on the cap on bankers' bonuses' [2013] JIBLR 363
Thüsing G,	'Das Gesetz zur Angemessenheit der Vorstandsvergütung' [2009] AG 517
Thüsing G/ Foster G,	'Nachhaltigkeit als Zielvorgabe für die Vorstandsvergütung' [2010] GWR 515
Velte P,	'"Nachhaltige" Vorstandsvergütung bei börsennotierten Aktiengesellschaften: Notwendige Einbeziehung von nichtfinanziellen Leistungsindikatoren?' [2016] NZG 294

Vetter E,	'Begrenzung der Vorstandsbezüge durch Hauptversammlungsbeschlus?' [2009] ZIP 1307
von Kann J/ Keiluweit A,	'Das neue Gesetz zur Angemessenheit der Vorstandsvergütung: Wichtige Reform oder viel Lärm um nichts?' [2009] DStR 1587
von Werder A/ Bartz J	'Corporate Governance Report 2014: Erklärung Akzeptanz des Kodex und tatsächliche Anwendung bei Vorstandsvergütung und Unabhängigkeit des Aufsichtsrats' [2014] DB 905
Wagner J,	'Nachhaltige Unternehmensentwicklung als Ziel der Vorstandsvergütung – Eine Annäherung an den Nachhaltigkeitsbegriff in § 87 Abs. 1 AktG' [2010] AG 774
Wagner J/ Wittgens J,	'Corporate Governance als dauernde Reformanstrengung: Der Entwurf des Gesetzes zur Angemessenehit der Vorstandsvergütung'[2009] BB 906
Wilsing H U/ Paul C A,	'Reaktionen der Praxis auf das Nachhaltigkeitsgebot des § 87 Abs. 1 Satz 2 AktG – Eine erste Zwischenbilanz' [2010] GWR 363
Wood P R,	'Legal impact of the financial crisis' [2008] 11 JIBFL 575

Books

Carmichael D R/ and others,	*Accountants' Handbook: 2 Volume Set/Special Industries and Special Topics* (10th edn, John Wiley & Sons 2003)
Burstein M L,	'Beyond the Banking Principle' in M L Burstein, Studies in Banking Theory, Financial History and Vertical Control (Palgrave Macmillan 1988) 63
Chen G,	'Talk about Foreign Commercial Banks Operating Risk Prevention of Reference and Enlightenment in Sweden for Example' in Jean Pierre Miahouakana Matondo and Xiaokang Zhao (eds), *2014 International Conference on Economic and Management (ICEM 2014)* (DEStech Publications Inc 2014)
Dauner-Lieb B,	'§ 87' in Martin Henssler and Lutz Strohn (eds), *Gesellschaftsrecht* (2nd edn, C H Beck 2014) § 87
de Bettignies H C/ Lepineux F,	Business, *Globalization and the Common Good* (Peter Lang Verlag 2009)

Depping A/ Walden D,	*CSR und Recht: Juristische Aspekte nachhaltiger Unternehmensfürhung erkennen und verstehen (Management-Reihe Corporate Social Respnsibility)* (Springer Gabler Verlag 2015) 88
Dewatripont M/ Tirole J,	*The Prudential Regulation of Banks* (The MIT Press 1994)
Döll M,	'Say on Pay: Ein Blick ins Ausland und auf die neue Deutsche Regelung' [2009] Institute for Law and Finance im House of Finance der Goethe-Universität Frankfurt working paper no 107, 11/2009 <http://www.ilf-frankfurt.de/fileadmin/_migrated/content_uploads/ILF_WP_107.pdf> accessed 11 May 2016
Dragomir L,	*European Prudential Banking Regulation and Supervision: The legal dimension* (Routledge 2012)
Francesco S,	*Value at Risk and Bank Capital Management: Risk Adjusted Performances, Capital Management and Capital Allocation Decision Making* (Academic Press 2010)
Freeman R E/ Valamuri S R,	'A new approach to CSR: Company Stakeholder Responsibility' in Andrew Kakabadse and Mette Morsing (eds), *Corporate Social Responsibility: Reconciling Aspiration with Application* (Palgrave Macmillan 2006) 86
Haas U,	'§ 62 Auflösung durch eine Verwaltungsbehörde' in Adolf Baumbach and Alfred Hueck (eds), *Gesetz betreffend die Gesellschaften mit beschränkter Haftung (GmbHG)* (20th edn, C H Beck Verlag 2013)
Hüffer U/ Koch J,	*Aktiengesetz: AktG* (12th edn, C H Beck Verlag 2016)
Ihrig H C/ Schäfer C	*Rechte und Pflichten des Vorstands* (Dr. Otto Schmidt Verlag 2014)
Issing O/ Bluhm M,	'Anforderungen an eine neue Ordnung der Finazmärkte' in Klaus J Hopt and Gottfried Wohlmannstetter (eds), *Handbuch Corporate Governance von Banken* (Verlag Franz Vahlen 2011) 77
Kort M,	'§ 87' in Klaus J Hopt and Herbert Wiedemann, *Aktiengesetz: Großkommentar* (4th edn, De Gruyter Verlag 2009)

Limpert B,	'§ 62 Auflösung durch eine Verwaltungsbehörde' in Holger Fleischer and Wulf Goette (eds), *Münchener Kommentar zum Gesetz betreffend die Gesellschaft mit beschränkter Haftung (GmbHG)* (2nd edn, CH Beck Verlag 2016)
Llewellyn D T,	*The Economic Rationale for Financial Regulation* (FSA Occasional Papers in Financial Regulation 1999)
Llewellyn D T,	'The Institutional Structure of Regulatory Agencies' in Central Banking, *How Countries Supervise their Bank, Insurers and Securities Markets* (Central Banking Publications 1999)
Nerlich J,	'§ 62 Auflösung durch eine Verwaltungsbehörde' in Lutz Michalski (ed), *Kommentar zum Gesetz betreffend die Gesellschaften mit beschränkter Haftung (GmbHG) II* (2nd edn, C H Beck 2010)
Ogus A I,	*Regulation: legal form and economic theory* (Clarendon 1994)
Padoa-Schioppa T,	*Regulating Finance: Balancing Freedom and Risk* (OUP 2004)
Ringleb H M	*Deutscher Corporate Governance Kodex: Kommentar* (5th edn, C H Beck Verlag 2013) para 722
Sachverständigenrat,	*Die Zukunft nicht aufs Spiel setzen: Jahresgutachten 2009/2010* (Bonifatius GmbH Buch-Druck-Verlag 2010)
Seibt C H,	'§87' in Marcus Lutter and Karsten Schmidt (eds) Aktiengesetz Kommentar (3rd ed, Otto Schmidt Verlag 2015)
Solozhentsev E D,	*Risk Management Technologies: With Logic and Probabilistic Models (Topics in Safety, Risk, Reliability and Quality)* (Springer Verlag 2014)
Spindler G,	*Münchener Kommentar zum Aktiengesetz: AktG* (3rd ed, C H Beck 2008)
Spindler G/ Stilz E,	*Kommentar zum Aktiengesetz: AktG* (3rd edn, C H Beck Verlag 2015)
Sweeting P,	*Financial Enterprise Risk Management (Internal Series on Actuarial Science)* (CUP 2011)
Valasquez M G,	*Business Ethics: Concepts and Cases* (3rd edn, Englewood Cliffs 1992)
van Gruening H/ Brajovic-Bratanovic S,	*Analyzing Banking Risk: A Framework for Assessing Corporate Governance and Risk Management* (3rd edn, World Bank Group Publications 2009)

von Eckardstein D/ Konlechner S,	*Vorstandsvergütung und gesellschaftliche Verantwortung der Unternehmnung: Zur Berücksichtigung der Gesellschaftlichen Funktion großer Kapitalunternehmen in Vergütungssystemen für die Mitglieder von Vorständen* (Rainer Hampp Verlag 2008)
Wasserer S,	'Neue Grundsätze für eine angemessene Vergütungspolitik – Zur Umsetzung der Vergütungsempfehlung der Europäischen Kommission im Rechtsvergleich Österreich und Deutschland' in Holger Altmeppen, Hanns Fitz and Heinrich Honsell, *Festschrift für Günter H. Roth zum 70. Geburtstag* (C H Beck Verlag 2011) 871
Weber M,	'§ 87' in Wolfgang Hölters (ed) *Aktiengesetz: AktG Kommentar* (2nd ed, C H Beck Verlag 2014
Weert F D,	*Bank and Insurance Capital Management* (John Wiley and Sons Ltd 2011)
Wolfers B/ Voland T,	'Sanierung und Insolvenz von Banken unter besonderer Berücksichtigung der Vorgaben des Verfassungs- und Europarechts' in in Klaus J Hopt and Gottfried Wohlmannstetter (eds), *Handbuch Corporate Governance von Banken* (Verlag Franz Vahlen 2011) 315
Wörner I,	*Europäische Bankenregulierung im Spannungsverhältnis zwischen Regulierungswettbewerb und Harmonisierungsbemühungen* (Nomos Verlag 2000)
Zöllner W/ Noack U,	*Kölner Kommentar zum Aktiengesetz: Kölner Komm AktG Band 6: §§ 291 – 392 und §§ 15-22 AktG* (3rd edn, Carl Heymanns 2004)

Statutory Provisions

- Aktiengesetz vom 6. September 1965 (BGBl I S 1089), das zuletzt durch den Artikel 1 des Gesetzes vom 22 Dezember 2015 (BGBl I S 2565) geändert worden ist <https://www.gesetze-im-internet.de/aktg/index.html> accessed 11 May 2016
- Charter of Fundamental Rights of the European Union [2000] OJ C 364/1
- Commission Recommendation (2004/913/EC) of 14 December 2004 fostering an appropriate regime for the remuneration of directors of listed companies [2004] OJ L385/55 and
- Commission Recommendation (2005/162/EC) of 15 February 2005 on the role of non-executive or supervisory directors of listed companies and on the committee of the (supervisory) board [2005] OJ L52/51

- Commission Recommendation (2009/384/EC) of 30 April 2009 on remuneration policies in the financial services sector [2009] L 120/22
- Commission Recommendation of 30 April 2009 complementing Recommendations 2004/913/EC and 2005/162/EC as regards the regime for the remuneration of directors of listed companies [2009] OJ L 120/28
- Commission Report (COM (2009) 114 final) of 3 March 2009 Communication for the spring European Council – Driving European Recovery Volume 1
- Commission Report (COM(2010) 285 final) of 2 Mai 2010 on the application by Member States of the EU of the Commission 2009/385/EC Recommendation (2009 Recommendation of directors' remuneration) complementing Recommendations 2004/913/EC and 2005/162/EC as regards the regime for the remuneration of directors of listed companies
- Deutscher Bundestag, BT-Drs 16-13433
- Directive 2004/39/EC of 21 April 2004 on markets in financial instruments amending Council Directive 85/611/EEC and 93/6/ECC and Directive 2000/12/EC of the European Parliament and of the Council and repealing Council Directive 93/22/EEC [2004] OJ L 145/1
- Directive 2009/138/EC of 25 November 2009 on the taking-up and pursuit of the business of Insurances and Reinsurance (Solvency II) OJ L 335/1
- Directive 2010/76/EU of 24 November 2010 amending Directives 2006/48/EC and 2006/49/EC as regards capital requirements for the trading book and for re-securitisations, and the supervisory review of remuneration policies [2010] OJ L329/3
- Directive 2011/61/EU of 8 June 2011 on Alternative Investment Fund Managers and amending Directives 2003/41/EC and 2009/65/EC and Regulations (EC) No 1060/2009 and (EU) No 1095/2010 [2011] OJ L 174/1
- Directive 2013/36/EU of 26 June 2013 on access to the activity of credit institutions and the prudential supervision of credit institutions and investment firms, amending Directive 2002/87/EC and repealing Directives 2006/48/EC and 2006/49/EC [2013] OJ L176/338
- Drittelbeteiligungsgesetz (DrittelbG)vom 18 Mai 2004 (BGBl I S 974), das zuletzt durch Arkitel 8 des Gesetzes vom April 2015 (BGBl I S 642) geändert worden ist (German law on co-determination for medium sized companies)
- European Parliament, Long-term shareholder engagement and corporate governance statement ***I: Amendments adopted by the European Parliament on 8 July 2015 on the proposal for a directive of the European Parliament and of the Council amending Directive 2007/36/EC as regards the encouragement of long-term shareholder engagement and Directive 2013/34/EU as regards certain elements of the corporate governance statement (COM(2014)0213 – C/-0147/2014 – 2014/0121(COD)) (Ordinary legislative procedure: first reading) <http://www.europarl.europa.eu/sides/getDoc.do?pubRef=-//EP//NONSGML+TA+P8-TA-2015-0257+0+DOC+PDF+V0//EN> accessed 11 May 2016
- Kreditwesengesetz in der Fassung der Bekanntmachung vom 9 September 1998 (BGBl I S 2776), das durch Artikel 4 des Gesetzes vom 11 April 2016 (BGBl I S 720) geändert worden ist

- Mitbestimmungsgesetz (MitbestG) vom 4 Mai 1976 (BGBl I S 1153), das zuletzt durch Artikel 7 des Gesetzes vom 24 April 2015 (BGBl I S 642) geändert worden ist (German law on co-determination for large companies)
- Regulation (EU) No 575/2013 of 26 June 2013 on prudential requirements for credit institutions and investment firms and amending Regulation (EU) No 648/2012 [2013] OJ L176/1
- Regulation of 4 March 2014 supplementing Directive 2013/36/EU of the European Parliament and of the Council with regard to regulatory technical standards with respect to qualitative and appropriate quantitative criteria to identify categories of staff whose professional activities have a material impact on an institution's risk profile [2014] OJ L 167/30
- Senior management arrangements, Systems and Controls (SYSC) March 2016 – how to add here? <https://www.handbook.fca.org.uk/handbook/SYSC.pdf> accessed 11 May 2016

Others

- Press release Council of the European Union for Economic and Financial Affairs of the 2911th Council meeting on 2 December 2008 <https://www.consilium.europa.eu/uedocs/cms_data/docs/pressdata/en/ecofin/104530.pdf> accessed 11 May 2016
- FSB, 'FSF Principles for Sound Compensation Practices' (FSB, 2 April 2009) <http://www.fsb.org/wp-content/uploads/r_0904b.pdf> accessed 11 May 2016
- FSB, 'FSB Principles for Sound Compensation Practices: Implementation Standards' (FSB, 25 September 2009) <http://www.fsb.org/wp-content/uploads/r_090925c.pdf> accessed 11 May 2016
- The Guardian, 'G20 leaders map out new economic order at Pittsburg summit' (The Guardian, 26 September 2009) <www.theguardian.com/world/2009/sep/25/g20-summit-economy-bonuses-deficits> accessed 11 May 2016
- EBA, 'Guidelines on sound remuneration policies under Articles 74 (3) and 75 (2) of Directive 2013/36/EU and disclosure under Article 450 of Regulation (EU) No 575/2013' (EBA, 21 December 2015) <https://www.eba.europa.eu/documents/10180/1314839/EBA-GL-2015-22+Guidelines+on+Sound+Remuneration+Policies.pdf/1b0f3f99-f913-461a-b3e9-fa0064b1946b> accessed 11 May 2016
- ESMA, 'Competition and choice in the credit rating industry: Market share calculation required by Article 8d of Regulation 1060/2009 on Credit Rating Agencies as amended' (ESMA, 18 December 2015) <https://www.esma.europa.eu/sites/default/files/library/2015-1879_esma_cra_market_share_calculation.pdf> accessed 11 May 2016
- Konrad-Adenauer-Stiftung, 'Welche Rolle spielten die Ratingagenturen bei der Entstehung der Finanzkrise?' (Konrad-Adenauer-Stiftung) <http://www.kas.de/wf/de/71.7074/> accessed 11 May 2016

- PRA, 'Strengthening individual accountability in banking and insurance – responses to CP14/14 and CP26/14' (Policy Statement PS 3/15, PRA 2015) <http://www.bankofengland.co.uk/pra/documents/publications/ps/2015/ps315.pdf> accessed 11 May 2016
- FSB Principles for Sound Compensation Practices (Implementation Standards) of 23 September 2009 <http://www.fsb.org/wp-content/uploads/r_090925c.pdf?page_moved=1> accessed 11 May 2016
- "SolarWorld AG" <http://www.solarworld.de/konzern/investor-relations/corporate-governance/verguetungsbericht/> accessed 11 May 2016
- Deutsche Bank AG <https://www.deutsche-bank.de/pfb/content/pk-rechtliche-hinweise.html?pfb_toggle=34735-34741> accessed 11 May 2016
- Commerzbank Aktiengesellschaft <https://www.commerzbank.de/portal/de/footer1/impressum/impressum_1.html> accessed 11 May 2016
- DZ Bank AG <https://www.dzbank.de/content/dzbank_de/de/footermetanavigation/footerlinks/impressum.html> accessed 11 May 2016
- BIS, 'Executive remuneration: Discussion paper' (Department for Business Innovation & Skills September 2011)
- Cannes Summit Final Declaration, 'Building our common future: Renewed collective action for the benefit of all' [2011] <http://www.g20.utoronto.ca/2011/2011-cannes-declaration-111104-en.html> accessed 11 May 2016
- FSB, 'Implementing the FSB principles for sound compensation practices and their implementation standards' [2015] FSB Fourth progress report, 15 <http://www.fsb.org/wp-content/uploads/FSB-Fourth-progress-report-on-compensation-practices.pdf> accessed 11 May 2016
- Julia Maues, 'Banking Act of 1933, commonly called Glass-Stegall' Federal Reserve History <http://www.federalreservehistory.org/Events/DetailView/25> accessed 11 May 2016
- EBA, 'EBA Report on the application of Directive 2013/36/EU (Capital Requirements Directive) regarding the principles on remuneration policies of credit institutions and investment firms and the use of allowances' [2014] EBA Report from 15 October 2014 <https://www.eba.europa.eu/docuents/10180/534414/EBA+Report+on+the+principles+on.pdf> accessed 11 May 2016